Doll Fashionistas

Sewing stylish dolls and their wardrobes

Ellen Lumpkin Brown

Doll Fashionistas

Sewing stylish dolls and their wardrobes

Ellen Lumpkin Brown

Cincinnati, Ohio

www.mycraftivity.com

Connect. Create. Explore.

fw
F+W PUBLICATIONS, INC.

Other fine Krause Books are available from your local bookstore, craft supply store, or fabric store. Visit the publisher at www.fwmedia.com.

13 12 11 10 09   5 4 3 2 1

DISTRIBUTED IN CANADA BY FRASER DIRECT
100 Armstrong Avenue
Georgetown, ON, Canada L7G 5S4
Tel: (905) 877-4411
DISTRIBUTED IN THE U.K. AND EUROPE BY DAVID & CHARLES

Brunel House, Newton Abbot, Devon, TQ12 4PU, England
Tel: (+44) 1626 323200, Fax: (+44) 1626 323319
Email: postmaster@davidandcharles.co.uk

DISTRIBUTED IN AUSTRALIA BY CAPRICORN LINK
P.O. Box 704, S. Windsor NSW, 2756 Australia
Tel: (02) 4577-3555

Library of Congress Cataloging in Publication Data

Brown, Ellen Lumpkin
 Doll fashionistas : sewing stylish dolls and their wardrobes / Ellen Lumpkin Brown.
   p. cm.
 Includes index.
 ISBN-13: 978-0-89689-712-0 (pbk. : alk. paper)
 ISBN-10: 0-89689-712-5 (pbk. : alk. paper)
 1. Dollmaking. 2. Doll clothes--Patterns. 3. Soft toy making. I. Title.
 TT175.B76 2009
 745.592'21--dc22

                        2008033496

Edited by Amy Jeynes
Designed by Rachael Smith
Production coordinated by Matt Wagner
Illustrations by Hayes Shanesy
Photos by Eugene Knowles except as follows:
  Photos by Christine Polomsky: pages 2, 4, 6, 8, 17 (bottom), 22, 41 (bottom), 43 (top left, bottom left), 60, 62, 66 (bottom), 70, 75, 82, 92, 94, 95, 107 (right), 108
  Photos by Buddy Scalera: pages 37, 38 (top), 43 (top right), 68 (left), 81, 85 (left), 86, 87, 88 (top left, top right), 90, 91 (top right, bottom right)
  Photos by Allison Brown: pages 55 (bottom left), 72, 84, 88 (bottom), 91 (top left, bottom left), 104, 107 (left)

745.5922
Br
c.3

Metric Conversion Chart		
To convert	to	Multiply by
Inches	Centimeters	2.54
Centimeters	Inches	0.4
Feet	Centimeters	30.5
Centimeters	Feet	0.03
Yards	Meters	0.9
Meters	Yards	1.1

About the Author

Ellen Lumpkin Brown has been making felt dolls since 1999. A mostly self-taught doll maker, she designs original heirloom-quality dolls and amazing doll fashions. Ellen and her dolls have been featured at www. quilterstv.com and in *Soft Dolls and Animals Magazine*. Through her online shop, The Doll Loft (www. TheDollLoft.com), Ellen loves to share her passion with others.

Ellen lives in South Orange, New Jersey, with her husband and three sons, who support the Doll Loft enterprise by assisting with everything from product testing and design to manufacture and marketing.

Acknowledgments

I have been blessed with loving support from my husband, Allison; my three sons, Nicholas, Aaron and Hampton; my brothers; my brothers- and sisters-in-law; my nieces and nephews and now great-nephew; and my mother- and father-in-law who have passed on. My dear friends from around the world also gave me endless encouragement. Their belief in me made this all possible. Thank you.

I also want to offer heartfelt thanks to a special group of people whom I have never met. They come into my life via television, the Internet, books and magazines. Their work has been a constant source of inspiration to me. To my mind come Mary Engelbreit, Sue Hausmann, Louise Cutting, Eleanor Burns, Elinor Peace Bailey, Donna Dewberry, Carol Duvall, Martha Stewart, Tim Gunn, Judith Licht, B. Smith, Martha Pullen and all their fascinating guests. Thank you so much.

Last, I owe special thanks to Sue Ann Taylor, a brilliant and visionary woman, for introducing me to Krause; and to Nancy Zieman, my hero.

Dedication

I dedicate this book to my mother, Georgia Lumpkin, who, on many a long summer afternoon when I could no longer think of anything to do, said, "Open up my box of odds and ends and make something."

Contents

Introduction

What is a fashionista? Fashionistas are the stylish people in the front-row seats at the Fashion Week shows in Paris, Milan, Hong Kong, Johannesburg and New York . . . but a fashionista is also anyone who loves fashion. Anywhere fashion is on display, fashionistas are there! Maybe you know a fashionista, or maybe you are one. I design original dolls, and my dolls are fashionistas because they love to wear the latest and greatest that the fashion world has to offer.

Designing dolls is a wonderful way to indulge your passion for fashion. In this book and its accompanying DVD, I'll show you how to make your own extraordinary custom dolls. Anyone can do it, from young to old and from beginning seamsters to advanced.

First, you'll learn an easy way to sew, stuff and assemble the parts of the doll. I'll teach you my paint-by-numbers method for creating fantastic faces. You'll learn how to add dimension and fabulous curves to your doll by sculpting the face and body with a needle and thread.

Next comes the clothing. I'll walk you through an easy, step-by-step process to create your own one-of-a-kind doll fashions with gorgeous fabrics, cool closures and fun trims and embellishments. With my techniques, you'll be able to create truly unique, sublime designs. You can even use these techniques on your own clothing!

Don't worry; making these dolls is easy, and you'll develop or advance sewing skills that will stay with you for a lifetime. Best of all, you won't be limited to the dolls or doll clothes that you find on store shelves. You can express your imagination and make something totally unique. You can be inspired by the latest fashion trends, or you can create your own fashion statement. Your finished dolls will reflect your style, creativity and spirit.

Seeing is believing—so all of this is demonstrated on the DVD that accompanies this book, where Nancy Zieman and I show you how to make dolls step by step.

Join Doll Crafters the World Over!

Dolls existed in the earliest civilizations and have been made from every conceivable material: wood, stone, paper, plastic, bark, bone, gourds, shells, fruit, leather, clays, porcelain, rubber, vinyl and, of course, cloth. Cloth dolls like the ones in this book, with movable limbs and removable clothing, date back to 600 B.C. When you make a doll with your own hands, you are joining an ancient tradition.

It's not surprising that cultures worldwide share a love of dolls. Dolls are often the most memorable and beloved gift a young girl receives. Dolls are best friends; they comfort us. When children play with dolls, they are practicing for parenthood. A doll with a special costume can remind us of a far-away homeland or help us preserve the memory of a special event in our lives. Heirloom dolls give us a tangible connection to our ancestors who passed them along to us.

Dolls tell history; dolls bind us together. They are truly magical. Once you experience the magic of making your first doll, you'll be hooked!

Through this book, I hope to share my love of sewing, design and the incredible experience of doll making. I hope you will visit my website, www.thedollloft.com, and email me photos of your creations! I'll post them in the gallery section of my site so that you can share your creation with everyone in the Doll Loft family!

Enjoy creating these little marvels. Let your creativity and spirit flow into your doll. Each doll will be a little piece of you!

—Ellen Lumpkin Brown

CHAPTER ONE

Tools of the Trade

It is important to select the right tools, fabrics, pens, pencils and paints to produce a good result. Poor-quality materials will give inferior results and will generally frustrate you.

Fortunately, though doll making may be addictive, it is not expensive! You probably have many of the tools and supplies in your home already. Anything you don't have can be found at your local craft store or fabric shop.

So start by assembling your supply kit, following the advice in this chapter. Having all your tools and materials at hand means you won't have to interrupt your creative play.

Choose the Right Tools and Materials

With the right tools, pens, paints and fabrics, you will achieve successful results even as a beginning doll maker. Quality materials will also be more durable. After all, your doll is a little part of you, and you want her to last for generations!

The tools described in this section have been chosen carefully because they get the job done. Happily, even with high quality products, it is not expensive to make *Doll Fashionista* dolls and fashions. I recommend these brands because I've had success with them; feel free to experiment with various brands to find your favorites.

SEWING MACHINE

Sewing machines range from inexpensive miniature straight-stitch machines to computerized models with hundreds of stitches and embroidery patterns built in. Rest assured, you can make my dolls with just about any type of sewing machine. When I designed the dolls in this book, I was using the good old Kenmore that my father purchased for me when I was fourteen years old. That dear machine has three stitches: straight, stretch and zigzag. That's more than enough to make *Doll Fashionista* dolls!

SCISSORS

If you're a complete beginner, inexpensive scissors are fine to start with, but the blades will wear out quickly, and you will probably need to replace the scissors before long. Once you get comfortable with sewing, purchase the best scissors you can afford; you won't regret it! To protect your investment, use your sewing scissors only for cutting fabric—never paper! Nothing will dull them more quickly than that. For a quick sharpening, snip a few times through several layers of aluminum foil. You can have your scissors professionally sharpened at the hardware store.

Doll Making Tools and Supplies

Steam-A-Seam 2

Steam-A-Seam 2, made by The Warm Company, is a wonderful fusible web product that allows you to join fabric pieces without sewing. Pressing with a steam iron makes the bond permanent. Steam-A-Seam 2 is great for areas that are difficult to manipulate on the sewing machine, such as narrow hems. It's also excellent for attaching ribbon trims and other embellishments.

Fabric Pens

Pens specifically designed for fabric are colorfast and will not bleed or run. Great choices include Micron, Marvy, DecoFabric, Zig, and the queen of all pens, Copic Pens. Copic pens come in a seemingly endless variety of shades and are specifically designed for precise, smooth and vivid applications of color.

You'll definitely need fabric pens in black, brown, white, red and pink. Later, you may wish to add blue, green, violet, gray and other eye colors. Choose a fine or medium tip; broad tips are usually too wide for doll facial features.

Watercolor Pencils

You'll use watercolor pencils to add color to facial features. Watercolor pencils are essentially dry watercolor in pencil form. You can dip the tip in water and "paint" on the doll's face for dark, bold color, or you can use it dry for lighter, softer shades. You can also use a dry pencil on wet felt; the color will blend and bleed in interesting ways.

Watercolor pencils are available in art and craft supply stores or from online sources (see the Resources list on page 122). Derwent and Faber Castell are two good brands.

Oil-Based Colored Pencils

Oil-based colored pencils are softer than watercolor pencils; they provide good coverage and strong,

Art Ware: Pens, Pencils, Pastels and Paints

vibrant color. Oil-based pencils are also great for shading larger areas on the doll's face. Be sure you are getting oil-based colored pencils and not wax-based. Prismacolor and Koh-I-Noor are good brands.

FABRIC PAINT

There are endless choices for fabric paint. For my dolls, you'll need fabric paints only for eyes and lips, so get white plus some lipstick shades. A small squeeze bottle of each color is all you need; they'll last forever!

Plaid, Polymark, Scribbles and Delta are all fine fabric paints.

If you have other uses for fabric paint, then check out the fantastic color options offered by Jacquard and Lumiere, which come in larger bottles.

Another option is to buy acrylic paint and add textile medium to it to make it usable on fabric. Textile medium transforms acrylic paint into washable fabric paint that remains soft and supple after it dries.

WOODEN SKEWERS

We will use wooden skewers to paint facial features. You do not need paintbrushes; in fact, brushes can work against you on felt because the bristles tend to lift the nap of the felt and create an uneven finish.

Embellishments
You can embellish doll clothes with anything and everything! Some of my favorites, shown here, are buttons, embroidery floss, decorative threads, snaps, hooks and eyes, beads, rhinestones, lace, grommets and trims. Tip: home decorating stores carry an extraordinary range of trims!

What You'll Need

This list includes all the items you will need make the beginner doll in chapter 2. When you've advanced to the point that you are ready to try the intermediate and advanced doll techniques, you'll need a few additional items that will be listed in the appropriate chapters. You can pick up those items when the time comes.

SEWING TOOLS

- Sewing machine (straight and zigzag stitches and adjustable stitch length are the only necessary features)
- Iron
- Hand sewing needles
- 8-inch (20cm) jointing needle (available at sewing and craft shops)
- 2-inch (5cm) curved needle for attaching hair
- Straight pins
- 6-inch (15cm) sewing scissors
- 2-inch (5cm) embroidery scissors
- Seam ripper
- Tailor's chalk pencil

FACE-PAINTING TOOLS

- Fabric pens, fine or medium point: black, brown, white
- Watercolor pencils in eye colors
- Oil-based pencils Fabric paints
- Acrylic paint: white
- Powder blush for cheek color
- Powder eye shadow: cream or white
- Workable fixative

DOLL MATERIALS

- Chenille stems. If you can find long pipe cleaners, they are stronger and less expensive than chenilles (thank you, Patti Culea!).
- Extra-strong thread such as upholstery thread or buttonhole twist
- Yarn for hair (one skein 75 yards [70m] or more per doll)
- 100 percent wool felt (one-third of a yard per doll)
- Airtex or other high-loft Polyfil stuffing
- Weighted stuffing material such as Plastic Pellets by Fairfield Products
- Wooden chopstick for stuffing and turning
- Wooden skewers

- 1-inch (3cm) wood balls for doll knees (two per doll)
- Small funnel
- Stiff cardboard for making Hair Loom (page 37)
- 1-inch (3cm) buttons for jointing (four per doll)

CLOTHING MATERIALS

- A stash of fabric scraps, ⅛ to ½ of a yard or meter
- Old sweaters and jeans for recycling into doll clothes
- A sheet of Iron-On Fusible Web
- Regular-weight polyester sewing thread
- Hand needles
- Zippers
- Ribbon, ¼-inch and 1-inch (3cm)
- Embellishments of all kinds

Fabulous Felt

Two of My Felt Pioneers
Here are two early versions of my Fashionista dolls. Notice the straighter body (left) and the more complicated knee (right).

A Snippet of History

Felt, a nonwoven textile, is the world's oldest fabric, predating spinning and weaving. It dates back to 6000 B.C., with the earliest examples found on the Central Asian steppes. In general terms, felt is created when natural fibers containing protein become wet. The microscopic scales on the hairs lift and catch on each other, and the fibers become tangled. Some believe that felt was born when nomadic tribes in central Asia and Turkey noticed how sheep's wool became matted and began to use the matted wool for the soles of shoes.

Felt is still used the world over for everything from clothing and hats to toys, saddles and rugs. In southern Africa, it's used for warm blankets; in central Asia, it's used for the walls of portable dwellings called yurts or gers. There is no more versatile textile!

I love felt for making dolls! It is an amazing textile. The first time I saw bolts of felt in a multitude of shades that resembled human skin tones, I was hooked. I purchased every shade of brown, beige, pink, peach and warm gold that I could get my hands on!

When I started making dolls with felt, I was in for a series of wonderful surprises. I found that felt took stuffing well, resulting in a doll with a very smooth body. Felt also holds its shape better than other fabrics and takes needle-sculpting beautifully. Finally, felt takes inks, fabric paint and cosmetics in a wonderful way that allowed me to achieve a very lifelike look. Working with felt as doll skin is similar to painting on porcelain; you can achieve subtle textures and shad-

ows that make the doll look real. *Doll Fashionista* dolls are specially designed to take advantage of the incredible properties of felt.

Felt comes in a wide variety of textures and thicknesses and in every color of the rainbow. The queen of all felt is 100 percent wool felt. Pure wool felt is smooth, soft and sturdy all at the same time. Felt made from wool blended with other natural fibers, such as rayon, is another good choice that is somewhat more economical. Other fabrics such as tightly woven cottons or doesuede can be used, but 100 percent wool felt will give you the very best results, guaranteed.

Materials for Doll Hair

Over the last several years there has been an absolute explosion of choice in fibers for knitting, crocheting and needle arts. For doll makers, that means an extraordinary selection of yarns for doll hair. You'll find many choices at your neighborhood yarn shop, craft store or online.

FIBER CONTENT
Yarn for doll hair can be silk, alpaca, rayon, wools, polyesters, blends, cottons, metallics, even bamboo! Any fiber type will work.

WEIGHT OR THICKNESS
Yarn comes in a wide range of weights. For best results, I recommend yarn in the following categories: fingering weight; sport weight; worsted weight; or bulky weight. Other yarns are either too thin or too heavy for doll hair.

COLOR
Almost anything goes when it comes to color, but here are a few tips:

- Variegated yarn will result in a more realistic look than yarn that is just one color. The exception is black yarn. Plain or metallic black yarn is just fine for doll hair.
- Yarn with flecks of gray or white will resemble gray or salt-and-pepper hair.
- If a yarn has green in it, the hair will look as though something is growing in it.

Yarn Colors for Natural-Looking Hair
There's a wide range of ash-toned and golden-toned browns and tans that make wonderfully realistic doll hair. Bouclé yarns, with their built-in kinks and curls, are great for curly hair, but you can also take straight yarn and curl it. I'll show you how in chapter 6.

"Fantasy" Hair Colors
If it suits your doll's fashion sense, there's no reason you can't choose colors such as pink or purple for hair. And you don't even have to use yarn! This doll's casual side-parted 'do is made of ½-inch (13m) silk ribbon with pinks and purples.

Choosing Fabric for Doll Fashions

When selecting fabric, give consideration to the following characteristics.

COLOR

- Don't feel limited to traditional "dolly" clothing colors. Try sophisticated colors: rich, dark, daring shades such as slate, navy, black, magenta and everybody's favorite—chocolate! Try brights such as fuchsia, lime, turquoise and true red.
- Seek inspiration for color combinations in nature. You can find so many unexpected and wondrous color pairings just by going outdoors and looking around you!
- Get free expert color advice by looking at magazines, advertisements, and fabric prints. Remember, magazines, ad agencies and fabric makers all have professional graphic designers working for them. Put their experience to work for you!

PRINTS

Proportion is important when choosing print fabrics for doll clothing. You can select smaller prints or larger ones, but generally, the main feature of the print should be no larger than 6 inches (15cm). A print that is much too big can overwhelm your clothing design.

PATTERNED FABRICS

Be aware that fabrics with plaids, stripes or one-way nap will take a bit more fabric and planning during cutting if you want the stripes or nap to match across seam lines.

DRAPE

Think about the garment you are making. Do you want it to flow? To stand out stiffly? To have a soft finish or a crisp finish? These are all affected by what is called the fabric's drape. Make sure that your fabric matches the finish you have in mind.

WEIGHT

Fabrics of different weights and textures are fun to work with. Feel free to mix and match unusual textures! Some tips:

- Light to medium weight fabrics are best for doll clothing.
- Very heavy fabrics are generally unsuitable, but they might work for a simple straight skirt.
- Slippery fabrics such as satin or shimmery knits are easier to sew when the fabric has been stabilized. Stabilizers, available at your favorite fabric store, can be sewn or ironed on. One simple

Get Inspired
These skirts, created from upholstery fabric, were inspired by a Prada advertisement I saw in a magazine!

The Three Rules of Fashionista Design

1. **Relax!** I'll show you how to create totally cool doll clothing with scraps, fat quarters, used clothing and embellishments.
2. **Try everything!** The patterns in this book are so quick and easy, you'll have plenty of time and energy to play.
3. **There's no such thing as a mistake!** Don't be dismayed or feel stuck if something doesn't come out just the way you intended. Think of it as a new design possibility . . . or, if you prefer to try again, that's okay too.

way to stabilize a very lightweight fabric is to iron a lightweight, wash-away stabilizer to the wrong side of the fabric. After the garment is complete, just dip the garment into warm water to dissolve the stabilizer, then hang the garment to dry.

STRETCH

All the sweater patterns in this book are designed for knit fabrics with some stretch. There is also a jean skirt on page 58 that can benefit from using stretch denim, which allows for a snug fit without pulling. Other than those projects, stretch fabric is not required.

SOURCES FOR FABRICS

- Old clothes are wonderful raw material for doll clothes! Many of my doll clothing designs use old blue jeans. Old wool sweaters are especially fun because they can be "felted," a process described in chapter 5. The felting process converts the knitted material into a thick, non-raveling fabric with all kinds of fashion possibilities.

- The hems and other details on old clothing can serve other purposes for your doll fashions. For example, the knitted cuff of a sweater sleeve can become a chic waistband for a doll sweater. There are no limitations! Let your imagination come out to play!

- Of course, you'll also love shopping for fabrics at your local craft and sewing shops or online. See the Resources section on page 122 for some ideas.

Look to the Color Wheel

The color wheel is a simple but marvelous tool that can help you mix and match colors for fantastic results.

Color families are the colors that are next to each other on the color wheel—they will go together nicely.

Complementary colors are colors that are opposite each other on the color wheel. Using these together makes both colors "pop."

Tints (lighter) and **shades** (darker) are what you get by adding white or black to a color. In design, lights look lighter next to darks, and darks look darker next to lights. You can use this in your clothing design: for example, a dark color can separate and accentuate two lighter colors.

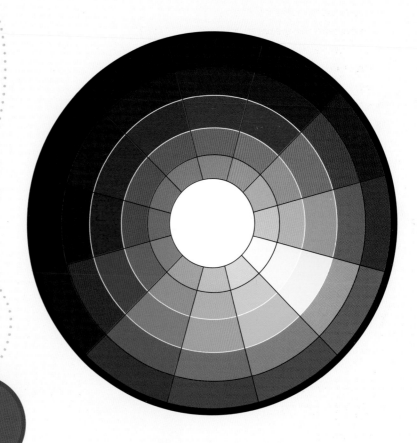

Doll Maker's Pincushion

In this project, you'll create your own doll maker's pincushion. This pincushion is both pretty and practical. It is oversized to hold all of your extra-long doll making needles, and when you make it, you'll get to practice stitching and turning; stuffing the pincushion using the chopstick, hand sewing with the ladder stitch; and, if you want, adding embellishments, trims or even needle sculpting. This pincushion makes a great gift for anyone who sews or wants to sew!

You probably have on hand all of the notions and supplies you need, even if you haven't yet assembled your doll maker's toolkit (page 15). So let's get started sewing!

Seam Allowances in This Book

Unless otherwise specified, the projects in this book assume a ¼-inch (6mm) seam allowance. That means you can simply use the side of the machine's presser foot as your guideline for sewing. Couldn't be easier!

WHAT YOU'LL NEED

MATERIALS

- Scrap of tightly woven fabric, enough to cut two pieces measuring 9" × 5" (3cm × 13m)

- *Note: Old jeans work great; non wovens such as felt are also a nice choice. Do not use knits for this project; they will stretch too much.*

- Regular cotton or polyester thread in a color that matches the fabric

- Extra-strong thread for attaching embellishments

- Polyfil stuffing

- Soft embellishments such as embroidery floss, felt, yarn, lace, rickrack or other fabric trims

- *Note: Hard embellishments such as buttons or beads are not the best choice for a pincushion because you'll have to avoid them when pushing in your pins.*

TOOLS

- Chopstick
- Darning or embroidery needle
- Scissors

1. Cut the Fabric

Cut your fabric scraps into two pieces 9" × 5" (23cm × 13cm). If you are using old jeans, just cut out a section of the leg as shown here, leaving the side seams intact.

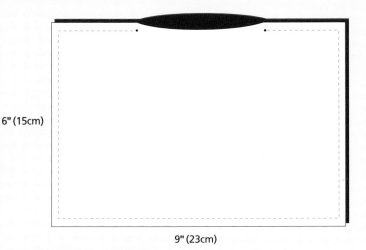

6" (15cm)

9" (23cm)

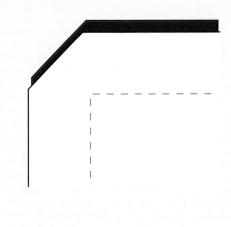

2. Machine-Stitch

Thread your sewing machine with matching thread. Put the scraps right sides together. Stitch on the open sides leaving a ¼-inch (6mm) seam allowance. Leave a 4-inch (10cm) opening for turning.

3. Clip Corners

If you are using a heavy fabric such as denim, clip the corners close to the stitching to remove excess bulk. Be careful not to snip through your stitching!

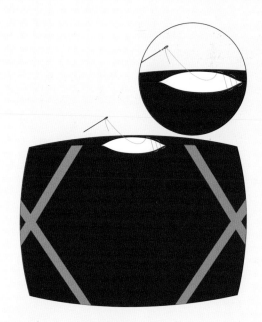

4. Turn

Turn the project right-side out through the opening you left. Smooth seams and push out corners with the chopstick. Add stuffing by small handfuls, using the chopstick to push stuffing into the corners. Stuff the pincushion very firmly so that it will hold your pins and needles in place well.

5. Close, Then Embellish

Thread a hand sewing needle and sew the opening closed using the ladder stitch (see Appendix F, page 125).

Using strong thread, attach soft embellishments such as embroidery, lace or felt flowers.

To make felt flowers, simply cut an easy flower shape out of one or two colors of felt, then stitch the felt onto the pin cushion by hand. Use embroidery floss and the stem stitch (see Appendix F, page 125) to create a stem and leaves for the flowers.

That's it! You now have your own one-of-a-kind pincushion!

CHAPTER TWO

Make Your First Doll

Now, let's get started with your first doll! When you make this doll, you will learn how to work with the felt, how to stuff the doll, how to use my easy template to paint the face, how to make yarn hair, and how to assemble your creation. You will also do a little beginning needle sculpting to add dimension to the doll.

Remember, no two dolls are alike. Your doll will be unique and one of a kind!

Your first doll will use the arm with the basic mitten-shaped hand. You'll get to choose your own yarn for a basic short hairstyle. This doll will be the foundation for the skills you'll learn in later chapters!

Stage 1: Body and Head

Doll bodies are made differently than garments. Compare the basic sequence of steps for each:

How Garments Are Made	How Doll Bodies Are Made
1. Lay out pattern pieces.	1. Lay out pattern pieces.
2. Cut out pieces.	2. Sew seams.
3. Sew seams.	3. Cut out pieces.

Notice the difference? For doll bodies, you stitch the pieces together first (leaving an unstitched opening for turning), then you cut them out, cutting ⅛ inch (3mm) outside the stitching and ¼-inch (6mm) from openings.

That small seam allowance is important; it allows the doll to plump nicely when stuffed. If you were to cut out the pieces and then sew—the way it's usually done—it would be much harder to achieve the narrow seam allowance. But with the doll maker's method, it's easy!

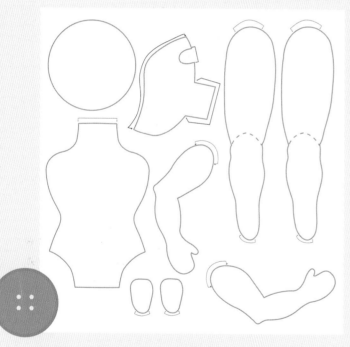

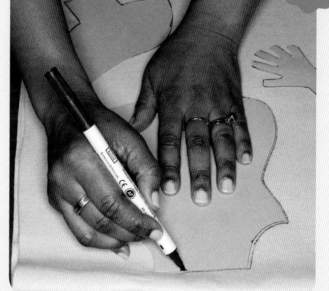

1. Place Pattern Pieces on Felt

Copy the pattern pieces from this book (pages 110-114), then cut out the pieces.

Fold the felt in half. Felt doesn't have a right or wrong side, so it doesn't matter which way you fold it.

Lay the paper pattern pieces on the folded felt. Since felt is not woven, it has no bias, so you can lay the pattern pieces on the felt in any direction.

2. Mark the Felt

Hold each pattern piece down with your hand, then trace it on the felt using tailor's chalk or a fine-tip pen. These lines are the stitching lines (unless I have indicated otherwise on the pattern), so they will not show once the doll is stitched and turned right-side out.

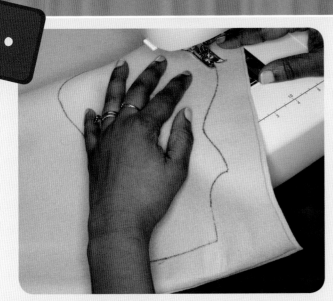

3. Sew the Body, Legs, Arms, Hands and Feet

Thread your machine and set it to a short stitch length of 20 stitches per inch. (The short stitch length will help you to stay right on the lines as you sew, which will give the doll a nice smooth shape.)

Remember, we're going to sew first, then cut out the pieces! Starting with the body, stitch along the traced lines. The pattern pieces show you where to leave openings for stuffing later; be sure not to stitch the openings.

Once you've stitched the body, proceed to stitch the legs, arms, hands and feet. Do not stitch the face or head yet.

WHAT YOU'LL NEED

MATERIALS

- Felt in skin color of your choice. Best: Wool felt. Typically 72 inches wide, folded and wrapped onto 36" bolt. Purchase $1/3$ yard (30cm) to make one doll. Less expensive alternative: Wool/rayon blend felt. Typically 36 inches wide, folded and wrapped onto 18-inch bolt. Purchase $3/4$ yard (70cm) to make one doll.

- Cotton or polyester thread to match felt

- Polyfil, one 32-oz. bag

- Weighted stuffing material such as Plastic Pellets by Fairfield Products

TOOLS

- Tailor's chalk or fine-tip pen

- Straight pins

- Sewing scissors

- Paper scissors

- Sewing machine

- Chopstick

- Small funnel

PATTERN PIECES

- From appendix A, page 110-114: Face, Head Back, Body, Legs, Feet, Arm With Simple Hand

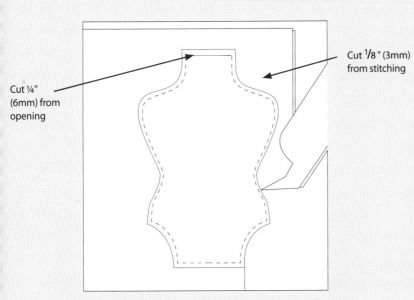

Cut ¼" (6mm) from opening

Cut ⅛ " (3mm) from stitching

4. Cut Out the Body, Legs, Arms, Hands and Feet

Cut out the body piece as follows: Cut ⅛ inch (3mm) from the stitching, and widen the margin to ¼ inch (6mm) at the unstitched openings. This will make it easier to turn the edges under when you are hand-sewing the pieces closed after stuffing.

Cut out the legs, arms, feet and hands the same way: ⅛ inch from the stitching, ¼ inch from the openings. Do not cut out the face and head yet.

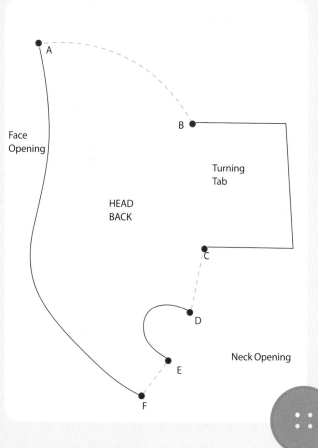

5. Trace and Stitch the Head Back

Now we're going to mark and stitch the head. (But don't cut it out yet.)

Trace the head back pattern piece onto the felt with your tailor's chalk or fine-tip pen. Mark points A, B, C, D, E and F on the felt, following the dots on the pattern.

Stitch the head back where indicated on the pattern— from A to B, from C to D, and from E to F—backstitching at the start and end of each seam. Make sure you have not stitched across the turning tab, the face opening, or the neck opening. Then stitch over the same seams (A to B; C to D; E to F) again for extra strength.

6. Cut Out the Head Back

Cut out the head back as follows:

- Cut ⅛ inch (3mm) from the stitching along the back of the head.
- Cut right on the lines for the face opening and the turning tab.
- *Stay stitch* (see appendix E, page 124) around opening where the head will be attached to the neck.

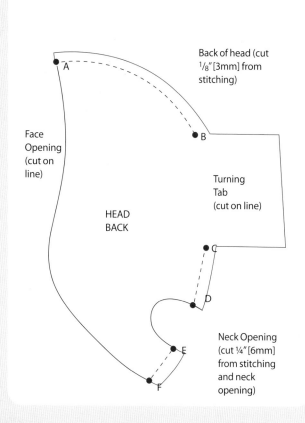

Extra Stitches Mean Extra Strength!

The backstitching, double seams, and stay stitching in steps 5 and 6 will keep the felt from stretching when you attach the head to the neck and stuff the head in later steps.

7. Cut Out Face and Pin to Head Back

Cut out one face piece. (Do not stitch on it yet.) Now, it's time to pin the face and head together. This looks tricky, but it is really quite easy. Just be patient and go slowly.

Open the back of the head with the right side facing you. Fold the face piece in half and fit it into the back of the head. Imagining the face as a clock face, pin it to the head back starting with four pins at 3, 6, 9 and 12. Then place additional pins all the way around. If the face is a little too large to fit, unpin it and stitch two lines of *basting* (see appendix E, page 124) around the face. Pull the threads gently to ease the fullness of the face and re-pin to the head back.

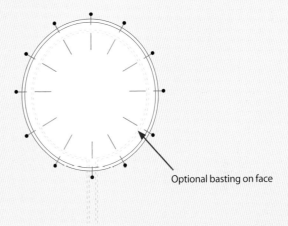

Optional basting on face

8. Stitch the Face to the Head

Machine-stitch the face to the head back, leaving a small seam allowance. Stitch slowly, with the same short stitch length we've been using all along (20 stitches per inch), and be patient. If you accidentally sew a tuck into the face, don't worry; I've done that lots of times. Simply pick up your seam ripper, take out a few stitches, then restitch.

Turn the head right side out through tab on the back of the head and set the head aside for now.

Turn the page, and we'll start stuffing the doll body!

9. Turn and Stuff the Body

Turn body right-side out, using a chopstick to smooth the curves and push out the corners. Stuff the body with poly-fil to the consistency of a ripe peach, stopping just below the waistline.

Use a funnel to add 1 cup (24ml) of plastic pellets to the doll's body. The pellets help give the doll her curvy shape, allow her clothes to fit properly, and provide weight.

Finish stuffing the body with polyfil. Stuff the shoulders and neck very firmly to support the weight of the head.

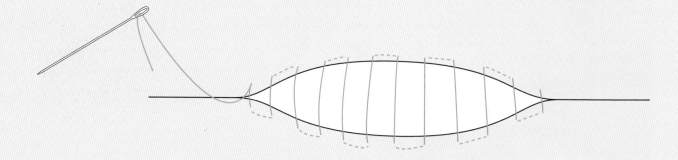

10. Close the Neck Opening

Thread a hand-sewing needle with a double strand of strong thread and use the *ladder stitch* (see appendix F, page 125) to close the neck seam.

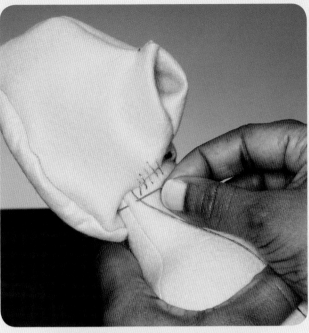

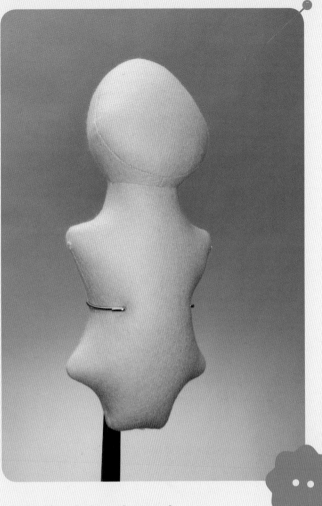

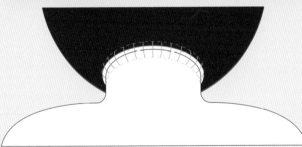

11. Attach the Doll Head to the Body

Using tailor's chalk or disappearing ink, mark a line on the doll's neck about ¾ inch (19mm) from the closing seam at the top of the neck. Slip the head onto the neck at the stay-stitched opening as shown. Thread a hand-sewing needle with a knotted double strand of strong thread, 18 inches (46cm) long. *Ladder stitch* (see appendix F, page 46) the head to the neck using small stitches about ⅛ inch (3mm).

Use the stay stitching line on the head and the line that you have just marked on the neck as your guides.

Pull up gently about every five stitches until the stitching disappears. Tie off. Repeat once more, if desired, for extra strength.

12. Stuff and Close the Head

Stuff the doll's head firmly and evenly through the remaining opening in the back. Go slowly and use small handfuls of stuffing. Make sure to stuff the chin area, and make sure the cheeks are plump and full. The head will appear pointed at the top, as you can see in the photo. Don't worry, the shape is correct and will be covered by the hair.

Trim the turning tabs, leaving ½-inch seam allowance. Tuck the seam allowance into the head, then *ladder stitch* (see appendix F, page 125) to close the opening.

On to the Next Stage: The Face

Congratulations! You've finished your first doll body. Take a breather; then, when you're ready, turn the page, and I'll show you how easy it is to paint a beautifully realistic face on your doll!

Stage 2: Paint the Face

Painting your doll's face is a lot of fun; this is the step that really makes the doll your own! After you plan the colors for the facial features, you'll choose your favorite eye, nose and mouth shapes. Then I'll show you how to position them with the Face Positioning Template (page 115) and paint them. The template will ensure that you place the facial features properly; it will also give you the basic proportions for each feature. Get ready to add the first touches of personality to your doll!

1. Brown (pen)
2. Light eye color (pencil)
3. Medium eye color (pencil)
4. Dark eye color (pencil)
5. Medium lip shade (pencil or, for dark-skinned dolls, fabric pen)
6. Darker lip shade (pencil or, for dark-skinned dolls, fabric pen)
7. White (pencil)
8. Brown (pencil)
9. White or cream (powder eye shadow)
10. Cheek color (powder blush) (Additionally: Black pen for pupils; white acrylic paint for whites of the eyes and eye highlights)

WHAT YOU'LL NEED

MATERIALS

- Felt scraps to practice on
- White acrylic paint
- Inexpensive cosmetics: powder blush for cheek color; white or cream powder eye shadow for highlighting
- Fine felt-tip pens: brown, black
- Oil-based colored pencils: white; brown; light, medium and dark eye color; two shades of lip color
- For dark-skinned dolls: fabric pens in two shades of lip color
- Workable fixative

TOOLS

- Wooden skewer
- Small, sharp scissors or craft knife
- Tailor's chalk or disappearing ink

PATTERN

- From appendix B, page 115: Face Positioning Template

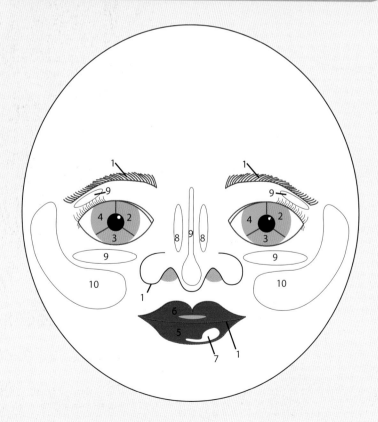

1. Choose the Colors

This numbered Face Painting Map shows which colors will go where. Assemble the paints and powders you plan to use.

Face Painting By the Numbers

This diagram shows you which colors go where. For full instructions, follow the step-by-step demonstration. Once you've painted lots of doll faces, the process will become second nature and you may only need to refer to this diagram for a refresher on the steps.

2. Practice Drawing Features

Referring to the examples on this page, practice drawing eyes, noses and mouth using a pencil and paper. When you are comfortable, move on to a scrap of felt.

How to Draw Eyes

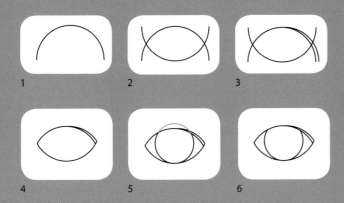

1 2 3

4 5 6

Square Eye

Draw the basic eye, then draw vertical lines just inside each corner of the eye and erase the points.

Almond Eye

Draw the basic eye, except:
- Make the upper lid a *single* heavy line.
- Tilt each eye so that the inner corners are slightly higher than the outer ones.

Basic Round Eye

A circle template, available at most art and craft stores, will help you draw accurate curves for your doll's eyes. You can also trace around coins or other round household objects. Try a 1-inch (25mm) diameter circle for the curves of the upper and lower lids, and a smaller circle for the curves of the iris.

How to Draw the Nose

You'll vary these shapes depending on how full or narrow you want the nose to be, but the basic steps are:
1. For the nostrils, draw two small triangles with rounded tips.
2. For the flares of the nose, add a C-shaped curve for the left flare and a reverse C for the right flare.
3. For the tip of the nose, draw a gently curving V between the nostrils.

How to Draw Lips

1. Start the upper lip by drawing two ovals or circles side by side, then one broader oval centered below them. For full lips, make the ovals fuller. For thinner lips, make the ovals flatter.
2. Draw a gently curving line between the top ovals and the bottom one, extending out a little to either side. This will automatically produce a soft smile!
3. Draw two curved lines over the top ovals to form the top lip. Draw a curved line under the oval to form the bottom lip.

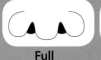

Full

Medium

Narrow

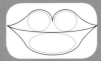

Full

Medium

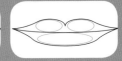

Thin

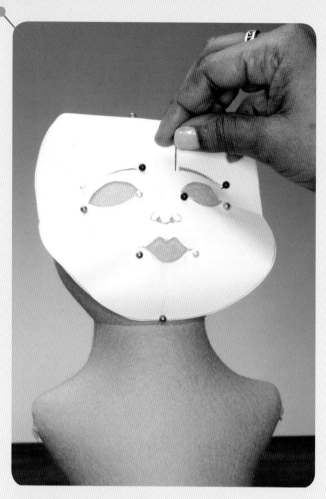

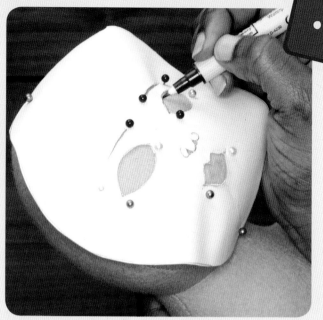

3. Pin the Face Template to the Head

Cut out the face template. Carefully cut out the eyes, eyebrows, nose and mouth using a small, sharp pair of scissors or a craft knife.

Pin the Face Template to your doll's face, lining up the seam markings on the template with the seams on your doll. Place pins at the corners of each feature to ensure that the template is lying flat against the face.

Practice Makes Perfect!

Before your paint on a doll for the first time, first practice drawing the facial features with pencil and paper. Then practice painting the features on felt scraps. When you have a feel for how the tools behave on felt, you can move on to paint on your doll's face.

One other tip: Use a light touch when coloring on fabric. Remember, you can always add more color, but you can't take it away.

4. Chalk the Features

Using tailor's chalk or disappearing ink, trace the doll's eyes, nose, eyebrows and mouth through the holes in the template. Sketch the features using a sharp chalk pencil. In this photo I'm using a pen, but if you're just starting out, you might want to use a chalk pencil first; that way you can brush away and redraw the lines until you are satisfied. Just be sure not to press too hard with a sharp tip and poke a hole in the felt.

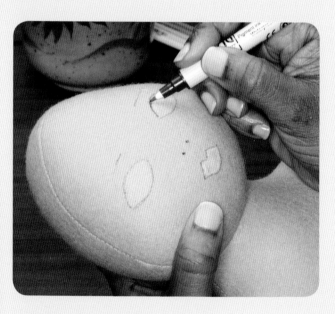

5. Outline the Features

Remove the template, then lightly outline the eyes, nose, eyebrows and mouth with a brown, fine-lined felt-tipped pen.

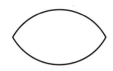
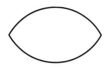

6. Outline the Eyes

Begin by outlining the eyes in brown colored pencil or a felt-tipped pen.

7. Outline Eyelids and Irises

With the same brown pencil or pen, create the eyelid by drawing a curved line just below the top lid line as shown. Draw in the irises, which should meet the eyelids as shown.

Outline the irises with a felt-tipped pen in a dark shade of your chosen eye color—brown, blue, green, hazel, violet, gray or whatever it may be.

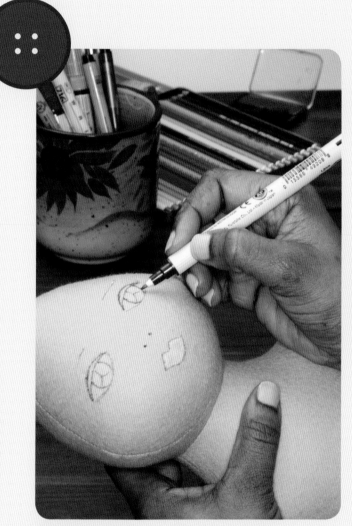

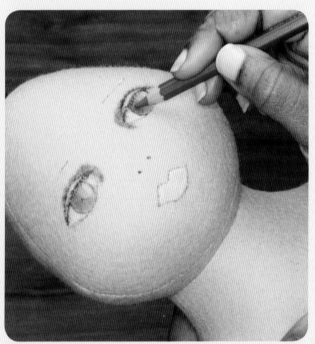

9. Color the Irises

Color in the irises with oil-based pencils as shown here and on the Face Painting Map (page 30). The right section of each eye should be the lightest shade of your chosen eye color; the bottom section will be the medium shade; and the left section will be the dark shade. (This mimics the look of realistic light.)

Outline the irises again with oil-based pencil in the darkest eye shade.

8. Detail the Irises

Use brown pencil or pen to add three lines radiating from the center of each iris.

10. Add the Eyelashes

Beginning at the outside corner of each eye, use the brown pen to draw eyelashes that curve slightly toward the nose. Start each stroke at the eyelid and pull up toward the eyebrow. Alternate between short and long lashes, and stop about halfway across the eyelid.

Also add two or three lashes toward the outside ends of the lower lids.

11. Add the Eyebrows

Now we'll create eyebrows by using a brown pen to feather in short straight lines on an angle. Start each line at the base of the brow and pull up, angling away from the nose. Make the brow strokes shorter as you work outward from the nose.

If you like, you can darken the eyebrows a bit by feathering black pen lightly over the brown pen.

12. Shade Around Eyes, Then Color the Pupils

Gently shade the inside and outside corners of the eyes using dark brown pencil to create depth.

Next, color in the pupil of the eye using either a black pen or a black watercolor pencil whose tip has been dipped in water. Using the tip of a wooden skewer, paint the whites of the eyes using white paint. After the white paint has dried (this will just take a few minutes), go over the outside of the iris with the darkest eye shade one last time.

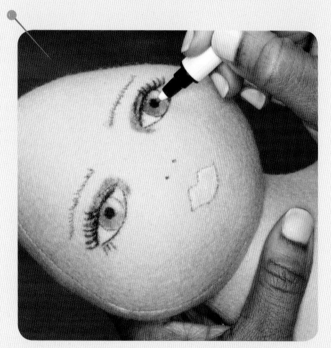

Use Care With Sharp Pencils!

Sometimes you need a fine point on your pencil, but be careful; a sharp point can tear the felt. Dull the sharpened point a little by running it across a piece of paper.

13. Draw the Nose

Draw two small triangles with rounded corners over the two nostril points using a brown oil-based pencil.

With brown pencil or pen, add the C-shaped curves to form the flares of the nose.

With brown pencil or pen, draw a soft, flat V between the two nostrils to form the tip of the nose. This line should be longer and a little sharper for a narrower nose.

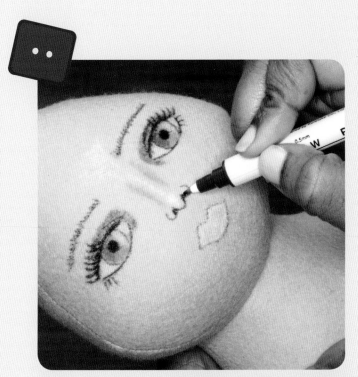

14. Shade and Highlight the Nose

Shade the nose by lightly drawing a straight vertical line from the top of the right flare to the corner of the right eye using a dry, soft brown watercolor or oil-based pencil.

Then, using a white oil-based pencil, fill in a small circle at the tip of the nose. Draw a line upward from the tip (about halfway up the nose). This line simulates light and makes the nose look three-dimensional.

Use a brown pen to touch up the lines around the nose if needed.

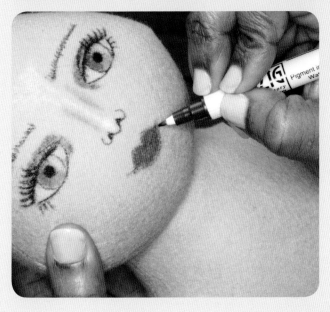

15. Outline and Color the Mouth

For dolls with light skin, outline the mouth using dark red or pink pencil. For dolls with dark skin, outline and fill in the lips with white pencil. (Yes, white! It will help the lip color show up better. Do not use white paint; you will not be able to color over it.)

Now it's time to color the mouth. If your doll has light skin, you will use a felt pen or a watercolor pencil; if she has dark skin, you'll use fabric pens. Color the top half of the mouth in a darker shade of red or pink and the bottom half with a lighter shade.

Use a brown pen to touch up the lines around the mouth if needed.

16. Draw the Lip Line

Using a light touch, draw in a simple lip line with brown pen to separate the top lip from the bottom lip as shown. This should just be a gently curving line to produce a soft smile.

17. Highlight the Lips

Using an oil-based colored pencil in a light shade of the lip color, highlight the bud of the top lip and the wide, full section of the lower lip. If desired, highlight the lower lip with a soft smudge of white oil-based pencil or a wet white watercolor pencil.

18. Highlights and Blush

Use a skewer and white fabric paint to add white highlights to the pupil of each eye. Pretending that each pupil is the face of a clock, place a small dot of white paint at 2 o'clock and another dot at 7 o'clock. I call these the wake-up highlights because they magically wake up the doll's eyes!

Blush the apples of the cheeks with your favorite blush color using inexpensive drugstore blush.

Use a very pale cream or light beige eye shadow with a light touch to highlight the area below the eyes where shown on the Face Painting Map (page 30). Add a bit more white or cream eyeshadow above the outside corners of the eyebrows. Lightly rub over the cheeks and forehead with a small scrap of felt to blend these colors to a natural finish.

That's it! To seal and preserve your doll's face, take her outdoors and spray the face with a workable fixative. (Definitely do this outdoors to minimize your exposure to fumes.)

Admire your work!

Stage 3: Hair

The hair is one of the most important elements of your doll; the hair will give her instant personality. Think about how a change of hair style or color can make a person look completely different. The same is true of dolls!

Short, long, wavy, kinky, curly, straight and frizzy are all fair play for doll hair. There are yarns for every mood, and the color choices are endless. Hand-dyed natural fibers make especially beautiful hair; their natural color variations make them resemble real hair with its natural "lowlights" or sun-drenched highlights.

Making and attaching yarn hair is easy. First, we will machine-stitch five to eight individual wefts of hair; then we will hand-sew them onto the doll's head.

WHAT YOU'LL NEED

MATERIALS
- Heavy cardboard
- Yarn for hair, 1 skein 75 yards (70m) or more
- Strong thread in a color matching the yarn

TOOLS
- Sewing machine
- 2-inch (51mm) curved hand-sewing needle

PATTERNS
- Hair Loom template, photocopied from page 116

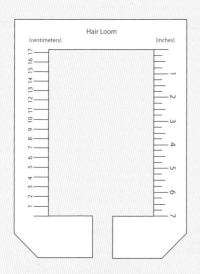

1. Make the Hair Loom
First, trace or glue the full-size Hair Loom template from page 116 onto a thick piece of corrugated cardboard, heavy art board, or foamcore. Cut out the Hair Loom using a craft knife or large pair of sharp scissors. (Don't use your sewing scissors!) Mark the long sides of the inside "window" of the Hair Loom in ½-inch (1cm) increments.

2. Fill the Loom With Yarn
First, tie the yarn onto the Hair Loom with a simple slip knot. Wind the yarn around the loom until you have a weft about 5½ inches (14cm) wide. The more yarn you use, the thicker your doll's hair will be. I like my dolls to have very thick hair, so I wind a lot of yarn on.

3. Stitch Across the Yarn
Thread your sewing machine and set it to about 15 stitches per inch. Stitch all the way down the middle of the weft, making sure to backstitch at the beginning and end. (Backstitching is important to ensure that no strands will come loose after you stitch the hair wefts to the head.)

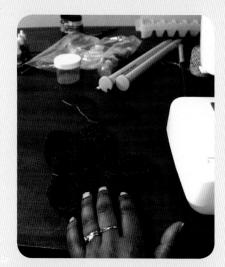

4. Remove the First Weft, Then Create More

Cut the knot you made in step 2 and slip the hair weft off of the loom.

Repeat steps 2 , 3 and 4 to create more wefts until you have five to eight of them, depending on how thick you would like your doll's hair to be. My dolls usually have six or seven wefts.

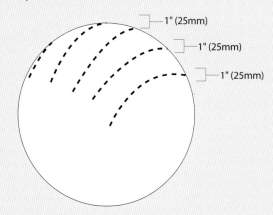

1" (25mm)

1" (25mm)

1" (25mm)

Place second weft abutting the first

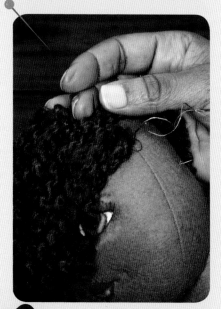

5. Attach the First Weft

Position the first weft on the head, centered just above the forehead. To center the weft on the head, fold it in half and position the fold along the back center seam of the head, then unfold the hair. Pin the weft in place, starting at the center seam and working toward the ends, just in front of the face seam so that the seam will not show.

Thread a curved needle with a knotted double strand of extra-strong thread, about 20 inches (51cm) long. Sew from one end of the weft to the other with a straight *running stitch* (see appendix F, page 125), taking stitches about ¼ inch (6mm) long and ¼ inch (6mm) apart. At the end of the weft, backstitch and knot off. You may wish to sew each weft twice for extra strength.

6. Attach the Remaining Wefts

Place the second weft right next to the first one, using the folding process described in step 5 to center the weft on the head. Stitch in place by hand. The reason we put the second weft right next to the first is to ensure a nice, thick appearance at the front hairline.

Position and sew on the remaining wefts, spacing each weft about 1 inch (25mm) from the previous one.

Stage 4: Arms and Hands

For your first doll, start with the basic arm pattern on page 112. It has a simple mitten-shaped hand. This hand is easy to sew, yet it can be placed in a variety of positions because of the pipe cleaner you'll be putting inside!

Cut out the arms making sure to leave the small tab at the top of the shoulder.

Turn the arm right side out. Use your chopstick (the smaller end) to gently press out the thumb.

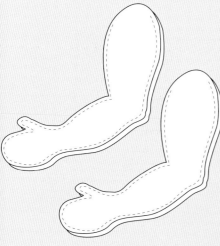

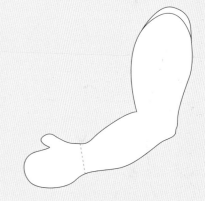

1. Review

At the beginning of this chapter (pages 25-26), you placed the pattern pieces for the arms on the felt. You then stitched around them and cut them out, leaving an opening for turning at the shoulder.

2. Turn the Arm and Add Pipe Cleaners

Turn the arms right side out. Use the smaller end of a chopstick to gently press out each thumb.

To create movable hands, fold two pipe cleaners (or chenille stems) loosely in half and push them gently into each hand.

3. Baste, Stuff and Close

Thread a hand-sewing needle and loosely baste across the wrists to keep stuffing from going into the hand. Stuff the arm firmly around the pipe cleaners/chenille stems using a chopstick. Stuff only the arms; do not stuff the hands.

Close the openings by tucking the seam allowances inside and sewing closed with the *ladder stitch* (see appendix F, page 125). Remove the basting at the wrists.

That's it for the arms and hands!

Stage 5: Legs and Feet

The legs have very nice articulated knees that are realistic looking and allow the doll to sit.

Thigh opening

Knee stitch line (unstitched to start)

Ankle opening

1. Stitch, Cut and Turn

At the beginning of this chapter (pages 25–26), you placed the pattern pieces for the legs on the felt. You then stitched around them and cut them out, leaving openings at both ends for turning. The curved line at the knee should not be stitched yet.

Turn the legs right-side out.

2. Stitch the Knee

Refer to the leg pattern; notice the curved stitching line at the knee. Using a chalk pencil, lightly draw this stitching line on the *outside* of each leg.

Machine-stitch the knee lines with a very short stitch length, about 25 stitches per 1-inch (25mm) to make sure that the socket curves gently as shown in the diagram. Stitch slowly and carefully; shorter stitches are more difficult to remove if you make an error.

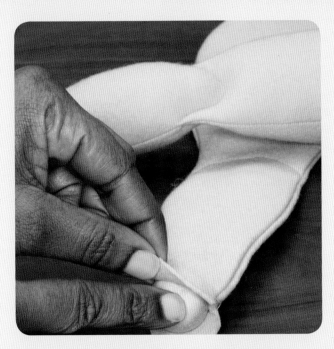

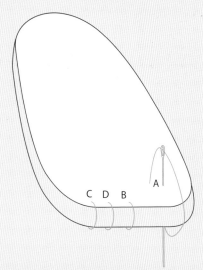

3. Use the Wooden Balls to Create the Knees

To make the knees, push a wooden ball through each ankle opening into the knee socket so that it fits snugly into the knee socket space. Stuff the lower legs firmly, making sure there is no unfilled space around the wooden balls.

Close the opening at each ankle with the *ladder stitch* (see appendix F, page 125).

Now, stuff the thighs loosely. If the thighs have too much stuffing, the doll will have very wide hips. Close the thigh openings with the ladder stitch.

4. Stuff the Feet and Needle-Sculpt the Toes

At the beginning of this chapter (pages 25–26), you placed the pattern pieces for the feet on the felt. You then stitched around them and cut them out, leaving openings at the heel for turning.

Turn each foot right side out and stuff lightly. Close the opening with a ladder stitch.

To make the toes, draw four short lines with chalk on the foot as shown in the diagram. Thread a needle with a long, knotted double strand of extra-strong thread. Enter the foot with your needle on the top of the foot where the foot will be attached to the ankle; this way, your knot will not show after the foot is attached. Exit at Point A on the top of the foot. Loop the thread to the underside of the foot and push the needle in at the bottom of the large toe. Pull gently to create the first toe.

Take a stitch inside the foot from point A to point B, and repeat the process. Repeat for the other toes at Points B, C and D. When all the toes are completed, exit the foot at the same spot where you entered, then knot off.

Sculpt the other foot the same way (be sure to put the big toe on the other side for the second foot!).

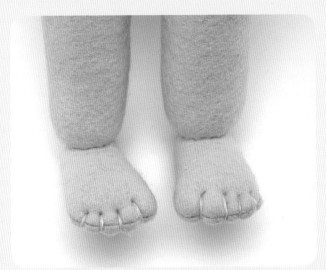

5. Attach Feet to Legs

Attach the feet to the ankles using the ladder stitch. Both legs are the same, so it doesn't matter which foot goes with which leg.

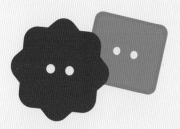

Stage 6: Assembly

As you can see, your first doll is almost complete! It's time to assemble her!

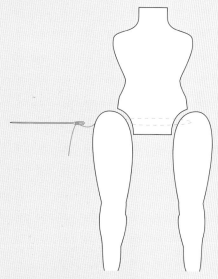

WHAT YOU'LL NEED

MATERIALS

- Yarn or embroidery floss to match felt
- Thread to match felt
- Two buttons, ¾" (14mm) in diameter
- Two buttons, 1¼" (31mm) diameter

TOOLS

- Jointing needle, 8 inches (20cm) long
- Hand sewing needle
- Scissors

1. Attach Legs to Body

Thread the long jointing needle with a double strand of embroidery floss or yarn about 24 inches (61cm) long. Lay the doll on her back facing you. Position the legs on either side, making sure that the feet are facing forward and that the big toes are on the inside.

Push the long jointing needle through one thigh; continue through the lower part of the body and into the other thigh, then out the other side as shown. Turn the needle and go back through the thigh, body and other thigh. Pull gently but tightly enough that the thighs have indentations at the top where the thread enters. Repeat at least three or four times for a strong connection, using a second piece of floss or yarn if necessary. The legs should be nice and snug to the doll's body, not loose or wobbly. Tie off.

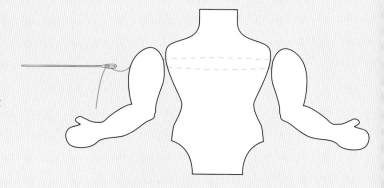

2. Attach Arms to Body

Use the same process as in step 1 to attach the arms to the shoulders. Pull the thread tightly; there should be indentations where the thread enters. Tie off. Repeat at least three or four times for a strong connection.

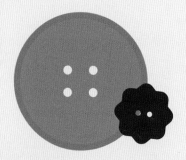

3. Test the Shoulder Joints

Test the arms as shown here. The arms should not be loose and should remain raised in a "hello" position when lifted.

4. Test the Leg Joints

The doll legs should move so that the doll can sit.

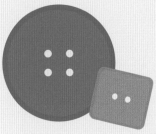

5. Hide Knots With Buttons

Cover knots and stitches with ¾-inch (19mm) buttons at the shoulders and 1¼-inch (31mm) buttons at the thighs.

And that's it! Admire your new, one-of-a-kind creation, your very own original doll!

CHAPTER THREE

Basic Doll Fashions

Dream! Design! Stitch! Shine!

Doll Fashionista dolls must wear fabulous clothing! This chapter will show you how fun and easy it is to make doll clothes. You will learn real sewing construction techniques when you make these clothes—techniques that you can also apply to making or personalizing your own clothes and accessories!

Doll Fashionista clothing patterns are designed to make up quickly and easily while providing a beautiful and professional result. Most patterns can be completed in less than two hours from start to finish . . . believe it! These pattern also have gorgeous finish with very little (if any) handwork. Once you are finished on the sewing machine, you are just about done!

The doll on the runway here is wearing our signature sundress with coordinating sandals. This dress is made from a beautiful silk fabric scrap that I found in the upholstery department. Because the dress only needs ½ yard or meter of fabric, it's easy to find really awesome fabric choices. The sandals can be coordinated with the dress by using a tiny piece of the fabric for the soles of the shoes or by using a matching ribbon for the ankle straps! Theoutfit makes up so quickly and easily that she can have a different outfit for each day of the week!

Signature Sundress

The first doll clothing project is this simple yet beautiful signature sundress. This little dress is made with just two rectangular pattern pieces, yet it can be created in many fantastic variations that you will see later in this book.

The directions for this dress include halter ties made of ribbon, but if you love strapless sundresses, omit the ties! If you think a drop waist is cool, sew it! Love lace? Trim your dress with loads of it! Your imagination is your only limit.

Remember the tips on page 18-19 about selecting fabric? If you're a first-time sewer, choose a medium-weight woven cotton fabric in an all-over print. Quilt shops have bolts upon bolts of fabric choices. You need only ½ yard (0.5m) to make a dreamy dress, so pick a fabric that you really love!

WHAT YOU'LL NEED

MATERIALS

- ½ yard (0.5m) of light-weight or medium weight woven cotton fabric
- Matching thread
- 24 inches of ¾- to 1-inch (19-25mm) wide ribbon for halter ties
- A length of ⅛-inch (3mm) wide ribbon to gather waist
- 15-inch or longer zipper, any color (contrasting colors are super!)

TOOLS

- Tailor's chalk pencil
- Sewing machine
- Sewing scissors
- Straight pins

Easy Ribbon Halter Ties
Ribbon makes a great design element for doll clothes. It comes in endless colors, and since it is already finished on both edges, the sewing involved is minimal.

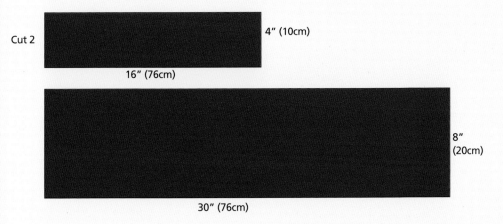

Cut 2

4" (10cm)

16" (76cm)

8" (20cm)

30" (76cm)

1. Cut Pattern Pieces

Fold your fabric right sides together, the way it came off the bolt. Position pattern pieces A and B on the fabric with the arrows running in the straight grain, as shown here.

Cut two rectangles 4" × 16" (10cm × 41cm) for the bodice and one rectangle 8" × 30" (20cm × 76cm) for the skirt.

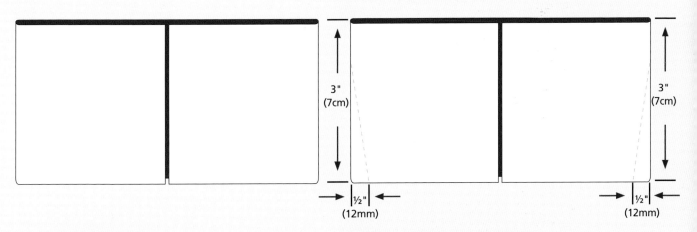

3" (7cm)

½" (12mm)

3" (7cm)

½" (12mm)

2. Fold the Bodice Pieces

Take one bodice piece and fold it in half to find the center of the long side; mark the center with a pin. Unfold the piece and lay it on your worktable with the right side up. Fold the side edges in so that they meet at the center mark. Finger-press these folds.

Repeat this step with the second bodice piece.

3. Mark and Stitch the Bodice Darts

Using tailor's chalk, mark two darts at the folds on the wrong side of each bodice piece, as indicated here.

Machine-stitch the darts from the wrong side using a regular stitch length (10 stitches per inch).

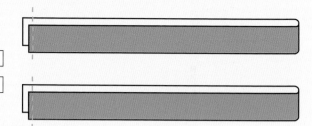

4. Cut Ribbon for Shoulder Ties

Cut two pieces of ribbon, each 12 inches (30cm) long.

5. Fold and Baste Each Tie

Fold each shoulder strap in half to 6 inches (15cm) in length. Baste the cut edges together (see appendix E, page 124).

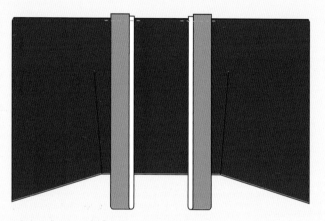

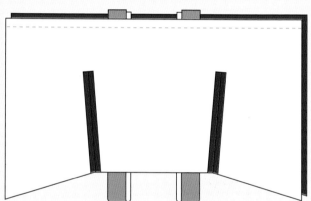

6. Baste Ties to Right Side of One Bodice Piece

Take one bodice piece and lay it on your table with the right side facing you. Position the ribbon ties on the long edge opposite the darts, matching the raw edges of the ribbon to the edge of the bodice fabric. The straps should be about one inch (25mm) toward the outside from each dart.

Baste the ties in place, stitching 1/8 inch (3mm) from the bodice edge.

7. Stitch Both Bodice Pieces Together

Lay the other bodice piece on top, wrong side up. Check that the ribbon ties are lying flat, neatly sandwiched between the two pieces. Stitch across, 1/4 (6 mm) from the edge, to secure the ties.

Set bodice aside.

Seam Allowances in This Book

When you stitch the pattern pieces together, you'll sew just about 1/4" (6mm) from the edge. You don't need to mark the seam line. Just use the edge of a regular presser foot as your guide. Every seam or hem in the book is 1/4" (6mm) unless indicated otherwise.

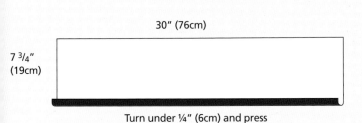

7 3/4"
(19cm)

30" (76cm)

Turn under ¼" (6cm) and press

6 3/4"
(17cm)

Turn under 1½" (4cm) and press

8. Begin the Skirt

Along one long side of the skirt piece, fold ¼ inch (6mm) of fabric toward the wrong side. Press. Stitch on the wrong side close to the edge to form a hem. This is now the bottom edge of the skirt.

9. Stitch the Skirt Hem

At the bottom edge of the skirt piece, fold 1½ inches (4cm) of fabric toward the wrong side. Press. Stitch on the wrong side close to the edge as shown.

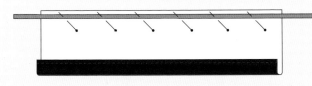

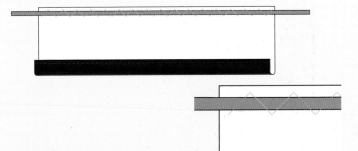

10. Ribbon Gathering

Cut a 36" (91cm) length of ⅛ inch (3mm) ribbon. Lay the ribbon on the wrong side of the skirt piece, ½ inch (12mm) from the top raw edge. Pin the ribbon in place.

11. Sew the Gathering Channel

Using a zigzag stitch 3mm wide and 8 stitches per inch, create a gathering channel by zigzagging over the ribbon, taking care not to stitch on the ribbon itself. Stitch slowly; the channel almost makes itself.

Try Ribbon Gathering!

The traditional way to make gathers is to sew two parallel lines of basting about ¼ inch (6mm) apart, then pull gently on the basting lines.

The ribbon gathering method is easier than the traditional method. It produces beautifully even gathers without any worries about broken basting threads. I learned this technique from watching *Sewing With Nancy*. Try it; I bet you'll love it!

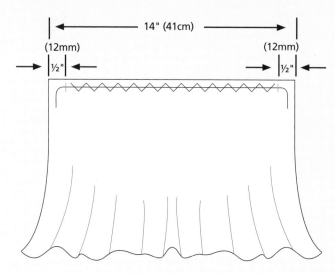

12. Gather the Skirt

Tack the ribbon down at one end only with a straight machine stitch ½" (12mm) from the edge, as shown. *Back-stitch* (see appendix E, page 124) to secure.

Pull the free end of the ribbon gently to gather the skirt until it is about the same width as the darted edge of one bodice piece, 14" (35cm). Hold the gathered skirt against a bodice piece and adjust gathers until the gathered edge is the same width as the bodice piece and gathers are evenly distributed. Leave ½" (12mm) ungathered at either end. Tack the free end of the ribbon ½" (12mm) from the edge as shown. The ribbon will remain in there permanently to support the gathers.

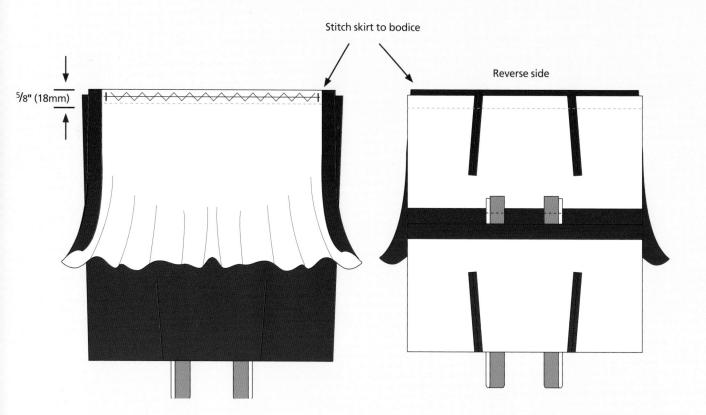

13. Stitch Skirt to Bodice

Pick up the assembled bodice you finished in step 7. Pin the skirt to the bodice with right sides facing. Turn the ungathered ends under, then stitch along gathered edge ⅝" (18cm) from the edge so that the gathering channel is completely within the seam allowance.

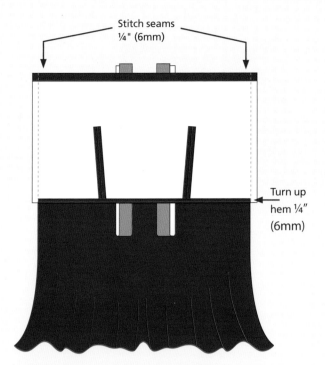

Stitch seams
¼" (6mm)

Turn up
hem ¼"
(6mm)

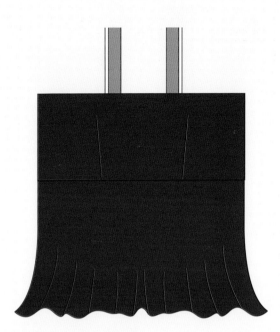

14. Stitch Bodice Pieces Together

On the raw edge of the bodice, fold a ¼-inch (6mm) hem toward the wrong side. Press. Fold the bodice pieces so that their right sides are together, making sure that the hem you just pressed is still folded and that it is at the bottom (as shown). Then stitch the side seams ¼ inch (6mm) from the edges. Sew these seams all the way off the edge of the fabric (that's easier than turning corners, and it will make a stronger seam, too).

15. Turn, Then Finish

Clip the corners of the bodice seams if needed to reduce bulk. Turn the bodice right side out. Press. *Edge-stitch* (see appendix E, page 124) the inside bottom of the bodice to the inside of the skirt to create a nice finish (this step can also be done by hand or with a narrow strip of Steam-a-Seam 2 fusible fabric bond, if you prefer).

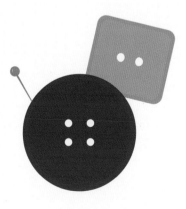

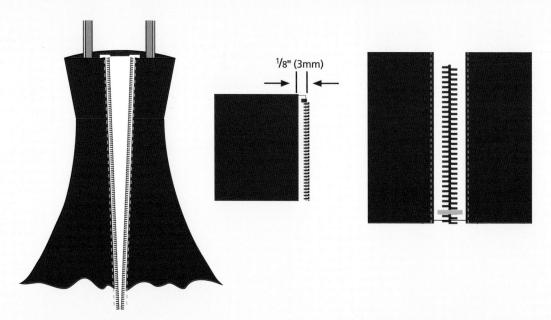

16. Position the Zipper

First, fully unzip the zipper. Line up the top end of the zipper with the top edge of the bodice and with the zipper teeth about 1/8" (3mm) from the back edge of the dress as shown. The zipper will show; feel free to use either a contrasting or coordinating zipper. Pin, spray baste or use fusible web to temporarily attach one of the zipper halves to the wrong side of the dress. The bottom of the zipper will extend beyond the hem of the dress. Don't worry; it is supposed to do that.

Stitch one of the zipper halves ¼ inch (6mm) from the edges of the back of the dress. Stitch on the right side of the fabric, making sure to backstitch at the top and bottom to ensure the zipper is securely attached.

With the zipper still open, pin the other side of the zipper to the wrong side of the other edge of the back of the dress. Zip up the zipper just to be sure it has not twisted. Unzip and stitch in place as you did the first half.

17. Create a New Zipper Stop

Zip the zipper up completely. Create a new stop for the zipper by making several stitches across the teeth at the bottom, either with a machine zigzag stitch or by hand. Cut off the excess zipper (save it to embellish another garment later).

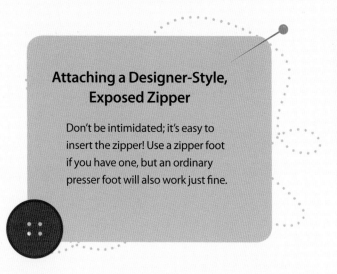

Attaching a Designer-Style, Exposed Zipper

Don't be intimidated; it's easy to insert the zipper! Use a zipper foot if you have one, but an ordinary presser foot will also work just fine.

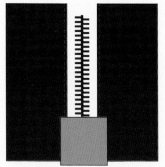

18. Conceal the Zipper Stop (Optional)

If you'd like to conceal the new zipper stop, cover it with a small piece of ribbon.

That's it! The dress is complete. No additional handwork is necessary. Try the dress on your doll!

Signature Sandals

These sandals are so quick and fun to make! They go well with the signature sundress.

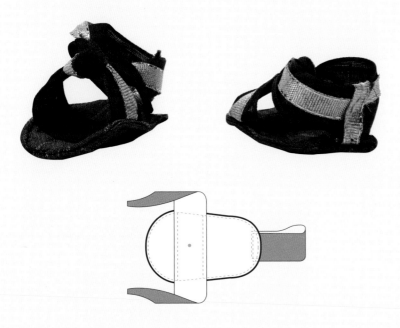

WHAT YOU'LL NEED

MATERIALS

- One piece medium-weight fabric, 6" (15cm) square
- One piece heavy fusible fleece, 3" × 6" (7cm × 15cm)
- 28 inches (71 cm) of narrow, $3/8$ inch (9mm) ribbon for ankle and toe straps

TOOLS

- Sewing machine
- Thread to match fabric
- Tailor's chalk pencil
- Sewing scissors

PATTERN

- Foot pattern, copied from page 112

1. Prepare the Sole

Position the rectangle of fleece on the wrong side of the sandal fabric, covering one-half of the square. Fuse the fleece to the fabric, following the manufacturer's instructions. Fold the fabric in half so that the right sides are together and the fleece is on the *outside*.

2. Make the Soles

Trace the sandal pattern piece twice onto the fabric sandwich to make two soles, then stitch on the trace lines, leaving a ½ inch (6cm) opening at each heel for turning. Cut out the soles, cutting ⅛ inch (3mm) from the stitching and ¼ inch (6mm) from the opening. Turn the soles right-side out with a chopstick. Push out the curves.

3. Add Heel Straps

Cut two 2-inch (5cm) lengths of ribbon. Take one of the pieces and fold it in half to form a loop. Tuck the raw ends of this piece into the turning opening on one of the sandals, leaving a loop of about ½ inch (12mm) for the strap. Tuck in the seam allowance and machine-stitch in place. Repeat this step for the other sandal. If desired, quilt the soles with straight diagonal stitch lines.

4. Add Toe/Ankle Straps

Cut two 12-inch (30cm) pieces of ribbon. If desired, sew a narrow hem at the raw edge of each end of the ribbon. Fold one of the pieces in half to find the center. Position this point of the ribbon right side down on the ribbon center point, as shown on the pattern piece above. Stitch the ribbon in place as shown. Repeat this step for the other sandal.

5. Finish

Topstitch (see appendix F, page 124) all the way around the edges of both soles, staying close to the edge; as you do this, stitch right over the ribbon straps.

Tie the toe straps with a loose square knot, then slip the ends of the ribbon through the loop of the heel strap and tie to fit. That's it!

Great Techniques: Uses for Ribbon

Ribbon is amazing! At your local craft store, you will find ribbons in beautiful colors and pretty prints: They will have drapey ribbons, crisp ribbons, narrow or wide ribbon. Because both of the edges of the ribbon are already finished, it is one of the easiest and quickest ways to make a bold statement on your doll's clothing. When using ribbon on your own clothing, make sure it is washable first.

Ribbon bows make quick embellishments.

Instead of elastic, run a long piece of ribbon through the waist casing of a skirt or pants, then tie the ends into a colorful bow. The bow can be on the front, back or side of the garment.

Soft silk ribbon can be used for incredible ribbon embroidery. I added upholstery trim with a decorative blanket embroidery stitch.

Ribbon can be used to make casual closures.

Ribbon can be added to the edges of zippers, snap tape, or hook-and-eye tape to create a fabulous design feature.

Ribbon accentuates the waist of this sundress.

Stitch, glue or fuse ribbon onto a garment to make a unique trim or to finish a raw edge.

This bodice is trimmed with a green ribbon casing. The waistband on the skirt is made of fabric, but it could just as easily have been made from a strong, crisp ribbon like grosgrain.

Skirt and Top From Recycled Clothing

Look in your chest of drawers for sweaters and jeans that you no longer wear. They make great raw material for doll clothes!

Often you can use the cuff of a sweater as the waistband for a doll skirt. A ragged hem on a pair of jeans can become the hem of a skirt with a well-loved, lived-in look. Buttons, trims, cuffs and collars all make chic, unique embellishment items for doll clothes, too.

WHAT YOU'LL NEED

MATERIALS

- Sleeves from an old knit sweater (Important: the knit must stretch in two directions)

- Leg from an old pair of regular denim jeans, or ¼ yard or meter of stretch denim

- Thread

- ½ yard or meter of ¼-inch (6mm) ribbon

- 11-inch (28cm) zipper

- Decorative trim for neckline, ⅓ yard or meter

TOOLS

- Marker

- Sewing scissors

PATTERNS

- Sleeveless sweater front and back, copied from page117

- Skirt front and back, copied from page 118

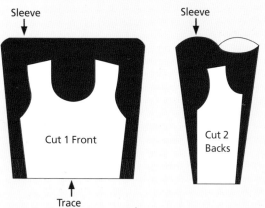

Sleeve

Cut 1 Front

Trace

Sleeve

Cut 2 Backs

SLEEVELESS SWEATER

1. Cut Out the Pattern Pieces

Cut off the sleeves from the sweater you've chosen to recycle. Cut each sleeve down the seam so that it's one layer of material.

Lay the sleeve material right-side up on your table, then lay the sweater pattern pieces on them so that the finished bottom edges of the sleeves become the bottom bands for the doll's sweater.

No pins are necessary; just hold each pattern piece down with your hand and trace it onto the right side of the material with a marker. Don't worry, the lines won't show!

Cut out two top backs and one top front.

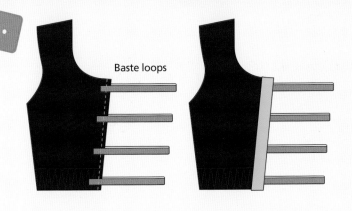

Baste loops

2. Stitch Hem and Ribbon Loops for Back Closure

Fold and press a narrow hem on each side of the sweater back. Stitch in place.

Cut eight 6-inch (15cm) pieces of ribbon. Fold them to make eight loops; these will become ribbon ties.

Position four loops on the right side of each sweater back piece, then baste in place as shown. Cover the raw edges on the right side with another piece of ribbon. *Top-stitch* (see appendix E, page 124) or fuse in place.

3. Stitch Shoulder Seams; Then Embellish, If Desired

Put the top backs and front right sides together. Stitch the shoulder seams. Remember, in this book, unless noted otherwise, seam allowances are ¼ inch (6mm); just use the edge of the presser foot as your guide.

Now is the time to add embroidery, chenille trim or other embellishment, if you'd like. It is easiest to embellish when you can lay the piece out flat, in other words, before the side seams are completed. Keep the embellishments 1 inch (25mm) from the side edges and ½ inch (12mm) from the top and bottom edges to allow for the seams and hems.

Back

4. Finish the Neck, Arm and Waist Openings

Finish the openings using any of the following methods:
- For a raw edge look, *edge stitch* (see appendix E, page 124) near the edges.
- For professional-looking narrow hems, first edge stitch (as for the raw-edge look) to prevent stretching. Then turn and press narrow (¼ inch [6mm]) hems. Baste the hems, then stitch them permanently using a stitch length of 10 stitches per 1-inch (25mm).
- Iron fusible bias tape along the edges.

5. Sew Side Seams

Stitch side seams right-sides together, then turn the sweater right-side out. Attach decorative trim with a few hand stitches. That's it! You've completed the top!

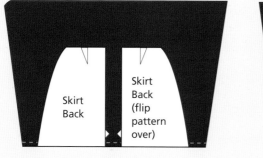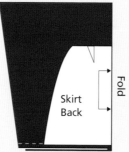

SKIRT

1. Cut Out the Pattern Pieces

Cut off the legs of the jeans you've chosen to recycle. Cut down one side seam of each leg so that you can spread the denim out.

Lay the denim right-side up on your table, then lay the skirt pattern pieces on them so that the finished bottom edges of the pant cuffs become the bottom hem of the doll skirt. Be sure to position the skirt front pattern piece on a fold as shown so that it is one piece when you cut it out.

Trace the skirt pieces onto the fabric with a marker, then cut out skirt front and backs.

2. Stitch Darts and Hems

Mark the location of the darts on the wrong sides of the skirt pieces, following the marks on the patterns.

Fold the first dart along the line with right sides facing, then stitch along the line. Repeat for the other darts.

Make a narrow hem at the top of each skirt piece. If you are not using old jeans, hem the bottom of each skirt piece, too.

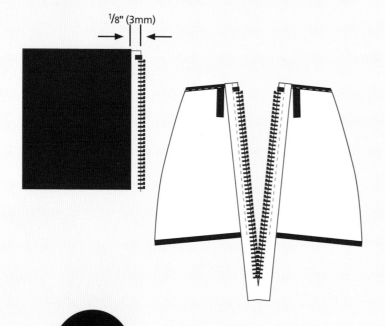

3. Insert the Zipper

Remember, inserting a zipper is easy! Press under ½ inch on each of the skirt back pieces at the back seam. Fully unzip the zipper and place it on the wrong side of the skirt with the pull-tab on the right side. Line up the top of the zipper with the top of the skirt. Hold one side of the zipper in place temporarily with Steam-a-Seam 2 or pins. The bottom of the zipper will extend well beyond the bottom of the skirt. Don't worry! We will cut it off later. Repeat this step with the other zipper half.

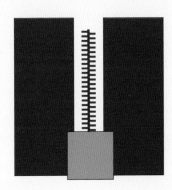

4. Stitch the Zipper

Attach the zipper as follows, starting and ending with a backstitch for strength.

Working from the right side of the fabric, stitch along one half of the zipper ¼ inch (6mm) from the edge of the skirt back.

With the zipper still open, pin the other side of the zipper to the wrong side of the other edge of the skirt back. Zip it up to make sure it's not twisted, then unzip and stitch the second half of the zipper in place as you did the first half.

5. Stitch a New Zipper Stop

Zip the zipper up completely. Make several stitches across the teeth of the bottom end of the zipper as shown, either with your machine's zigzag stitch or by hand. Cut off the excess zipper. Cover the new stop at the bottom of the zipper with a small piece of ribbon or a button as described in step 18 on page 52.

6. Stitch the Side Seams

Stitch the side seams of the skirt, right-sides together.

7. Turn and Press

Turn the skirt right-side out and press.

You've finished the skirt! Pair it up with the top on page 56. Perhaps you'd like to make another pair of sandals (page 53) to match this outfit.

When you're ready, turn the page to chapter 4, and I'll show you some intermediate doll-making techniques!

CHAPTER FOUR

Intermediate Doll Techniques

In this chapter, we advance to new territory! Now that you've mastered making the basic doll from chapter 2, I'll show you some new and exciting techniques that will make your next doll truly fabulous!

First, you'll learn how to do deep needle sculpting in order to add realistic-looking dimension to your doll's face. You'll learn an easy trick for creating shoulder-length hair. Finally, you'll learn how to make a doll hand with shapely fingers. The fingers will be able to change positions, wear rings, and even hold lightweight objects!

I love wide skirts. So I was thrilled when I saw a magazine advertisement for clothing by the famous Prada fashion design house, featuring dirndl skirts as the new must-have item for every fashionista's wardrobe!

My fashion-forward skirt, on the facing page, was made from scraps of upholstery fabric with a big, bold print. I paired the skirt with a simple sweater. I love the result!

Needle-Sculpted Face

Deep needle sculpting is the process of using a long needle and strong thread to actually shape the doll's face much as a sculptor molds clay. You will create cheeks, dimples and a special soft smile for your doll—all with a needle and thread!

Needle sculpting will be new to many readers, but it's not difficult; just go slowly and take your time. The part that requires the most practice and patience is finding the right exit point with your needle as you take the sculpting stitches from the back of the head to the front. The demonstration on the enclosed DVD will help you get it right with a little practice. By the time you reach the last sculpting point, you will be sculpting with confidence!

What You'll Need

MATERIALS

- Strong thread in a matching color. Upholstery thread or buttonhole twist will do.
- Doll with face painted per instructions in chapter 2
- Extra-strong thread to match doll material

TOOLS

- 5-inch (13cm) doll sculpting needle, available at most craft stores or from the Doll Loft website (www.TheDollLoft.com)

Needle Sculpting Adds Dimension and Depth
You can see here the dramatic difference that sculpting makes on a painted face. All it takes is small stitches at the eyes, nose dimples and mouth to create curves, shadows and an expression that makes your doll truly special.

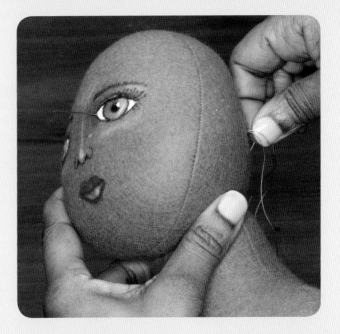

1. Begin Sculpting the Eyes

Make sure your hands are clean and free of lotions or oils (see "Clean Hands Are a Must," below).

Thread the doll sculpting needle with a 24-inch (61cm) double strand of extra-strong thread, knotted at the end.

Take a small stitch at the back of the head to anchor the thread.

2. Aim the Needle

Push the needle straight through from the back of the head toward the inside corner of the right eye. Adjust the needle until the point comes out right at that inside corner. Getting the needle to come out at the right place is the part of sculpting that takes a little time; just be patient.

Clean Hands Are a Must!

My needle sculpting technique is fool-proof because you will do the sculpting *after* you have painted the doll's face. That way, you are certain that the sculpting points are positioned where you want them.

Because you will be working on a finished, painted face, make sure your hands are squeaky clean and free of lotion or oil before you start sculpting to avoid smudges!

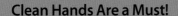

3. Pull the Needle Through

When the needle comes out at the inside corner of the right eye, pull it through.

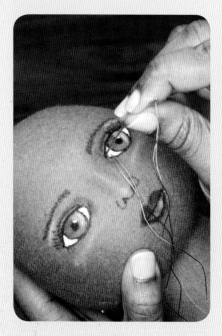

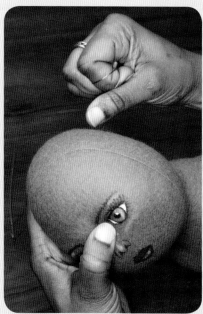

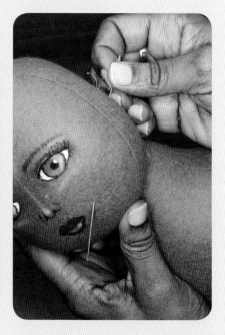

4. Push Needle Back Through

Push the needle back through the head very near the spot where it came out. The length of the stitch should be about ⅛ inch (3mm). Push the needle through and out the back of the head.

5. Tighten the Thread

To create an indentation at the corner of the eye, pull the thread gently while squeezing the head firmly between your thumb and forefinger. Pull the thread more firmly to create a deep indentation. By squeezing the head, you are taking some pressure off the thread and felt, which helps prevent tearing. Keep squeezing as you tie off the thread. (See the DVD for a demonstration.)

Repeat from step 1 at the outer corner of the right eye, then rethread your needle and sculpt the corners of the other eye.

6. Push Through at Cheek Point

To begin the first cheek dimple, push the needle in through the back of the head and exit at one of the dimple points marked on the template.

Important Sculpting Tip

After every two or three sculpting points, re-thread your needle with a new 24-inch (61cm) double strand of strong thread. Otherwise the thread may become so short, you'll have a hard time tying it off.

Optional: Sculpt the Nostrils

Sculpting the nostrils is optional. I find that they do not add as much dimension to a face as the other sculpting points.

If you'd like to do it, the technique is a little different. As with the cheeks, you will begin at the top of the head. Exit through one of the nostrils, take a small stitch, and return to the top of the head. Pull gently to create a slight indentation and tie off. Do not pull very tightly; this indentation does not need to be very deep. Most of the dimension in the nose is created in the face painting process.

7. Stitch and Pull to Create Cheek Dimple

Take a ⅛-inch (3mm) stitch, then push the needle up and out through the top of the head. Pull the thread while squeezing the cheek firmly upward on the dimple with your other hand to help form a nice full cheek.

8. Dimple the Other Cheek

Repeat steps 6 and 7 to form the other cheek dimple.

9. Sculpt the Smile

Doll Fashionista dolls are famous for their knowing, gentle smiles. To create the smile, push the needle in at the top of the head and aim for the corner of the mouth. Taking a small stitch, push the needle back in and then exit at the top of the head. Pull the thread gently to create a soft smile, then tie off. Repeat on the other corner of the mouth.

You now have a beautiful, fully sculpted doll face. Use your pens and pencils to go over the facial features once more. Re-outline the eyes, irises, nostrils and lips to ensure good definition; add more color if desired. Take the doll outdoors and spray the face with workable fixative.

Shoulder-Length Hair

In chapter two (see page 38) you saw how to attach hair horizontally from the front hairline all the way back. The result is a short hairstyle. If you'd like a longer style, it's easy to do; you just attach the last few wefts in a vertical rather than a horizontal fashion. Here's how!

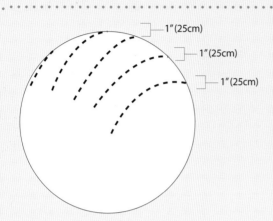

1" (25cm)

1" (25cm)

1" (25cm)

Horizontal Wefts Make Shorter Hair
When all the wefts are attached horizontally, they hang down the sides and create a short hairstyle.

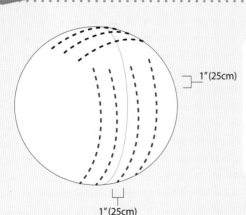

1" (25cm)

1" (25cm)

How to Position the Wefts for Shoulder-Length Hair
To make shoulder-length hair, you simply apply the wefts to the head in a different pattern. Start with two closely spaced wefts applied horizontally across the front hairline, just as before. Then attach the remaining five or six wefts vertically, as shown here. These vertical wefts hang lower than horizontal ones, creating a shoulder-length hairstyle for your doll.

Hands With Fingers

You made your first doll with simple, mitten-shaped hands. Now I'll show you how to create hands with shapely and graceful fingers. Stitching and turning fingers is a new challenge. Stitch slowly and patiently . . . you can do it!

I make a special finger-turning tool that is available at my website, www.thedollloft.com. Without a turning tool, it is time-consuming to turn the fingers. You can also improvise a turning tool by using a plastic straw and the blunt end of a skewer.

MATERIALS LIST

MATERIALS
- Long pipe cleaners (or regular chenille stems)

TOOLS
- Finger-turning tool (described at left)
- Small sharp scissors
- Chopstick

PATTERNS
- Arm with fingers copied from page 113

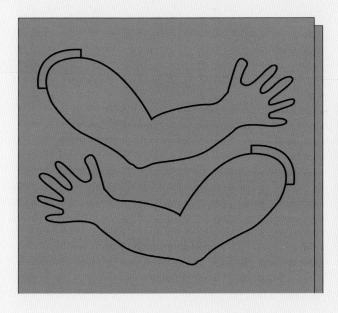

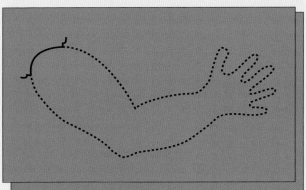

1. Trace the Pattern Onto the Felt

When tracing the pattern pieces on felt for your next doll body, refer back to the pattern tracing instructions on pages 24–25, except substitute the arm with fingers (pattern piece, page 113) for the arm with simple hand.

2. Stitch the Hands and Fingers

Stitch the pieces according to the instructions on page 25, except use the following tips when stitching around the hand and fingers:

- Reduce your machine's stitch length to about 22 stitches per inch; this way, you can stitch the fingers more accurately.
- Sew the hand and fingers slowly and carefully.
- Be sure to have at least two or three stitches in the little U between each finger so that the fabric doesn't pucker when turned.

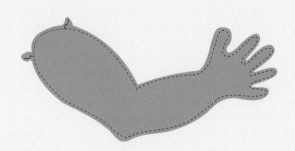

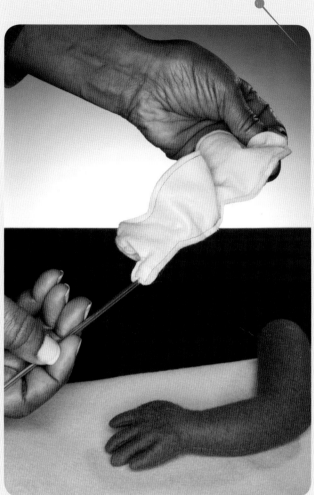

3. Cut Out the Arm

When you cut out the arm and hand, use these tips:

- Use scissors with short, sharp blades, such as embroidery scissors.
- Cut 1/16"–1/8" (2-3mm) from the stitching.
- Cut between each finger and make a tiny, tiny clip at the corner taking care not to cut through your stitching.

4. Turn the Fingers, Hand and Arm

To turn the fingers right-side out, you will need the two-part turning tool that is available at my website, www.TheDollLoft.com. It consists of a hollow metal tube and a solid metal rod. You can also improvise a tool using a plastic straw and the blunt end of a skewer.

Begin by pushing the hollow tube into one of the fingers. Use the solid rod to gently push just the tip of the finger into the hollow tube. The hollow tube holds the tip of the finger so that you can begin the turning process. Once you have the tip of the finger turned, remove the metal tube, then take the narrow end of your chopstick and gently push the finger the rest of the way into the hand. Repeat the turning tool process for the remaining fingers.

When all five fingers have been turned, use the larger end of the chopstick to gently push the entire hand out through the arm opening. Pull each finger gently so that it extends fully. Finger-press to relieve any tightness between the fingers.

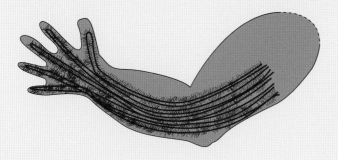

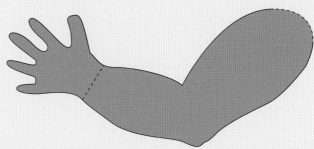

5. Add Pipe Cleaners

Now we'll add chenille stems or pipe cleaners to fill in the fingers and make them positionable.

Fold one pipe cleaner loosely in half, then push the folded end gently inside the arm all the way to the tip of the thumb. Repeat for the other fingers, working in order from thumb to pinky so that the fingers stay nice and neat. Press the long ends of the stems together inside the arm so that they stay together. When you are finished, the chenille stems or pipe cleaners will mimic the bone structure of a real hand and arm.

6. Baste, Stuff and Close

Thread a hand-sewing needle and loosely baste across the wrists to keep stuffing from going into the hand. Stuff the arm firmly around the pipe cleaners/chenille stems, using the chopstick to push the stuffing in. Stuff only the arms; do not stuff the hands.

Close the openings by tucking the seam allowances inside and sewing closed with the *ladder stitch* (see appendix F, page 125). Remove the basting at the wrists.

CHAPTER FIVE

Intermediate Doll Fashions

In this chapter, you will learn four exciting techniques: sewing scallops; needle felting; flouncing; and ways to create your own, unique buttons.

I learned about the needle-felting technique from *The Martha Stewart Show*. I made it my own by adding beads and crystals. Try the techniques in this chapter, then use them to jump-start your own creativity!

This outfit is inspired by the Xhosa women of South Africa. When I lived in South Africa, I saw Xhosa women when I was driving through the Eastern Cape province, and I remember being struck by their beauty, dignity and sense of style. These women were able to use just a few embellishments, bright, solid-colored fabric, black twill tape and buttons to create amazing clothing design. That was in the mid-1990s. I am now thrilled to see these treatments making their way into mainstream South African fashion!

Scalloped Hem

Here's a variation on the signature sundress from chapter 2, page 23. I'm going to show you how to sew scallops!

Normally, scallops are considered an advanced sewing technique, but when you use the doll maker's "sew first, cut second" technique, scallops are easy to do. After you've completed this scalloped dress hem, you might like to try scallops for the top edge of a bodice, too.

WHAT YOU'LL NEED

Everything listed for the signature sundress on page 46, plus:

MATERIALS

- A rectangle of the same fabric as used for the skirt, measuring 4" × 30" (10cm × 76cm), for the scallop facing (Piece C)

TOOLS

- A round flat object that is about 1.5 inches (32mm) in diameter—you can use a small saucer, a jar lid, a large coin, whatever you can find. This will be your marking guide for making the scallops.

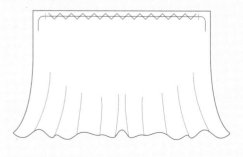

Completed bodice with ties (page 48)

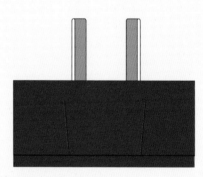

Skirt portion, gathered, no hem (page 49)

1. Begin the Dress

Turn to page 46 and work the signature sundress up to and including step 7 on page 48. Skip steps 8 and 9, then work steps 10 and 11.

30" (76mm)

3 ¾" (9mm)

2. Press a Hem

Press a narrow hem on the long edge of Piece C and stitch in place.

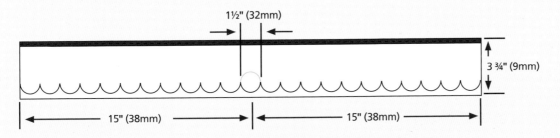

1½" (32mm)

3 ¾" (9mm)

15" (38mm)   15" (38mm)

3. Mark the Scallops

Fold Piece C in half lengthwise to find the center. Press gently at the midpoint or mark with a chalk pencil. Open the piece out. Working on the wrong side of the fabric, center your scallop guide at the midpoint. Draw a semicircle with the chalk pencil. Move the guide to the left end of the semicircle and draw another scallop. Repeat to the edge of the facing. Return to the center and complete another set of scallops starting at the right edge of the center scallop to the right edge of the facing fabric. You have just drawn in your stitching line! You may need to adjust the scallops at the back edge slightly so that they will match when the dress is complete.

Piece B

Piece C

⅝" (17mm)   ⅝" (17mm)

4. Stitch the Scallops

Put Piece C and the finished skirt portion from step 1 right sides together. Shorten your stitch length to about 15 stitches per inch (2.5cm). Sew slowly and carefully on your chalk stitching line. Stitch a ⅝th inch seam at the left and right edges of the skirt.

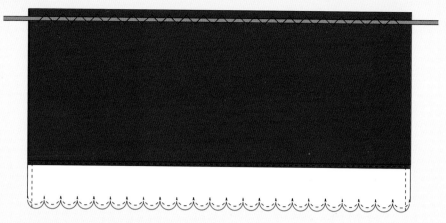

5. Trim the Scallops

Using small, embroidery scissors, cut away the excess fabric, leaving a very small ⅛th-inch (3mm) seam. Be careful not to cut through your stitching!

6. Turn Scallops

Turn the scallops right-side out; push them out and smooth them with your chopstick. Press the scallops using plenty of steam. If the points between each scallop are lumpy, turn wrong-side out and make a tiny, tiny clip right at the point. This will ease the pressure on the fabric. But again, be careful not to clip through your sewing.

Now, return to page 49, step 12, and proceed with the instructions to finish your sundress.

Variations on the Scalloped Edge

This same technique can be used with a triangle template to make a jagged dress hem or with a shallow curve to create a wavy hem. You can also embellish your scallops with buttons. Give that a try, too!

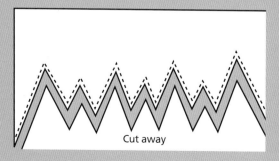

Cut away

Needle Felting; Beading

This pretty sweater is designed to be made from a used, ready-to-wear sweater that has been felted in the washing machine. You can felt any natural fiber, knitted fabric (wool is best) by washing it in hot water, then drying it in a hot dryer (the opposite of how you're supposed to treat a wool sweater!).

Felting is a great way to give an old sweater a new life. Best of all, the cut edges of felted wool will not unravel, so there is no need to line the sweater or finish its edges.

In this demonstration, we'll needle-felt some flowers and enhance them with beading.

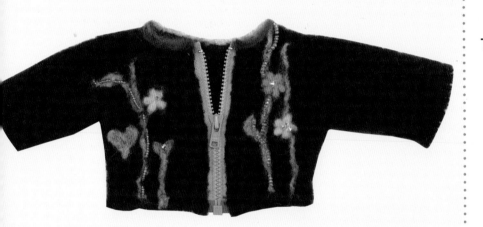

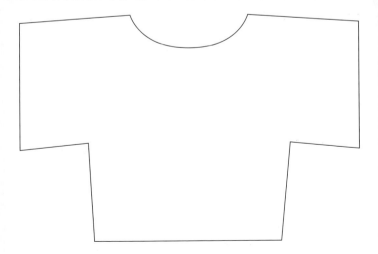

WHAT YOU'LL NEED

MATERIALS

- Small amount of wool roving or yarn
- Several colors of seed beads
- 4-inch (10mm) separating zipper
- Old wool sweater, felted by washing in soap and hot water, then drying in a hot dryer

TOOLS

- Felting needle
- Small block of sponge foam, available at craft or fabric stores; look in the aisle where the pillow forms are
- Beading needle
- Sewing scissors

PATTERN

- Long-sleeve sweater (page 119)

1. Lay Out and Trace the Pattern Piece

Cut your felted sweater open so you can lay the material out flat.

Position the sweater pattern pieces on the material. Hold the pattern piece down with your hand and cut around it. Repeat to cut out a second piece.

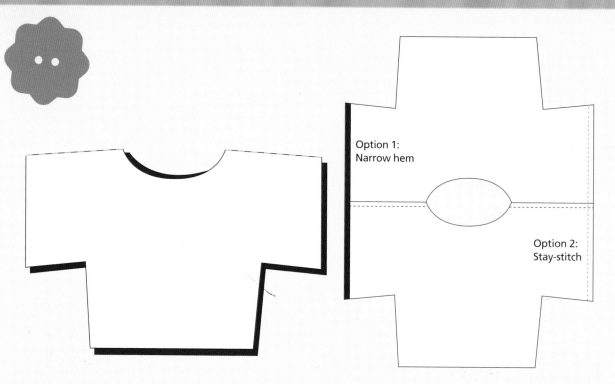

2. Shoulder Seams

Stitch shoulder seams together, using a stretch stitch and a stitch length of about 15 stitches per inch. Finger-press the seam open.

3. Sleeves

Stitch a narrow hem at the bottom of the sleeve, if desired. Since the felted sweater will not ravel, this step is optional. You can also *staystitch* the edge of the sleeve with a *stretch stitch* (see appendix E, page 124).

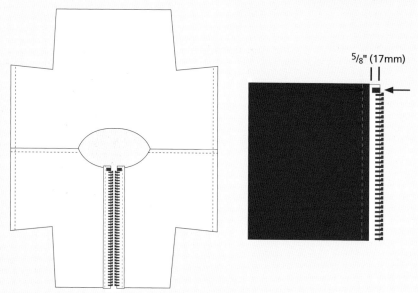

5/8" (17mm)

4. Cut Open the Front, Then Insert the Zipper

With your sewing scissors, cut all the way down one side of the sweater to create the front opening.

Unzip the 4-inch (10cm) separating zipper. Place the zipper halves on the wrong side of the front of the sweater with the right side facing out. Hand-baste in place. Carefully machine-stitch the zipper halves in place, keeping the stitching close to the front edge of the sweater.

Repeat for other side.

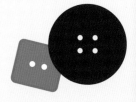

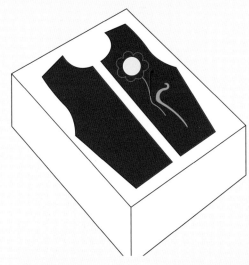

5. Needle-Felt a Design on the Sweater Front

This is a easy way to make a quick, bold statement through embellishment. Lay out narrow strands of wool roving on the sweater front in a pleasing pattern (flowers, hearts or whatever you wish). Place the sweater front on the small piece of sponge foam. (For the sake of clarity, I've left the sleeve areas and the sweater back out of the illustration.) Using the felting needle, repeatedly poke the needle straight up and down through the roving and the sweater fabric, using the needle to form and refine the shapes. Continue the felting process until the roving adheres to the sweater.

6. Bead the Design

To bead over the felting, thread the beading needle with a double strand of thread knotted at the end. Take an anchor stitch on the reverse side of the sweater front. Come up through to the front, pick up one or more beads with your needle, then stitch them onto the felted design until you are pleased with the result.

7. Side Seam

Place the right sides of the sweater together. Sew the side seam of the sweater and bottom seam of the sleeve in one long seam.

8. Finish

Turn sweater right-side out. Finish the neckline and hemline using either of the following methods:

- *Stay-stitch* (see appendix E, page 124) using a regular straight stitch (not a stretch stitch).
- Press a ¼-inch (6mm) hem on all raw edges, the neckline, front and bottom of the sweater. Stitch hem in place (you will need to leave a ¼-inch (6mm) allowance at the top and bottom of the zipper).

Skirt With Flounce

Here' you'll learn how to create a ruffle, or flounce, to use at the bottom of a skirt. The flounce is made in a coordinating or contrasting fabric. You will need a piece of fabric that is 4" × 31" (10mm × 79mm) inches to make the flounce. Pick what you like!

The trim for the skirt is ½-inch (12mm) wide. You only need ½ yard or meter, so select a pretty trim! Colored trims that contrast or coordinate work very well on this skirt.

The skirt top is made from stretch denim, which has Lycra woven into it, to give a snug fit.

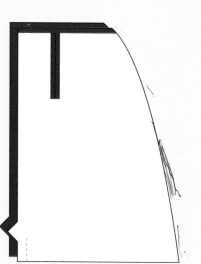

What You'll Need

MATERIALS

- Stretch denim, ⅓ yard or meter

- Lightweight cotton for flounce, one strip measuring 6" × 25" (15cm × 64cm)

- A pretty embellishment trim ½"–¾" (12mm × 19mm) wide

- Zipper, 5"–7" (13cm × 18cm)

TOOLS

- Tailor's chalk pencil or disappearing ink

PATTERNS

- Skirt front and back pieces, copied from page 118

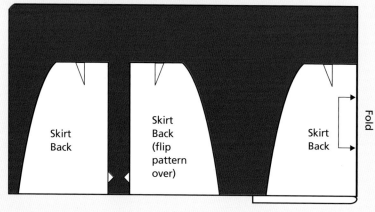

1. Cut Out Pieces

Lay the skirt front and back pattern pieces on the denim and trace them with disappearing ink. Cut out and mark the skirt darts with the disappearing ink. Stitch and press (do not trim) the darts on front and back of the skirt top.

Cut a strip of lightweight cotton 6" × 25" (15cm × 64cm) for the flounce (not shown).

2. Stitch Lower Back Seam

Stitch narrow hems along the top edges of skirt fronts and skirt back.

Put the two skirt backs together, right sides facing, and stitch the back seam only from the bottom edge to the notch.

3. Press Center Back Seam

Open the skirt back and press the seam allowances.

4. Position the Zipper

Unzip zipper (the zipper can be 5–7 inches [13–18cm] long, the excess will extend beyond the top of the skirt). Place bottom of the zipper at the notch on the skirt back seam. Pin in place or use a spray adhesive.

5. Sew Zipper

Sew zipper in place stitching on the right side of the fabric as shown. While the zipper is still unzipped, create a new zipper stop by hand-stitching several stitches across the zipper near the top on each side. Make certain that these stitches are strong and secure. Cut off the excess zipper and save it to trim another garment.

6. Sew the Flounce

Fold the flounce fabric right-sides together as shown. Stitch at both ends of the flounce.

7. Turn; Add Gathering Stitches

Turn the flounce right side out. Use a pin to gently pull out the corners. Press.

Zigzag-stitch a ribbon gathering channel, as shown in step 11 on page 49.

8. Gather and Attach the Flounce

Gather the flounce to fit the skirt.

Pin the flounce to the right side of the skirt. Stitch in place with a ½-inch (12mm) seam. Press. Trim the seam allowance of the flounce fabric to ¼-inch (6mm) to reduce the bulk of the gathers).

9. Add Trim

Now let's make the skirt really special! Cut your trim to fit the skirt. Pin trim onto right side of skirt covering the flounce seam. Stitch trim in place.

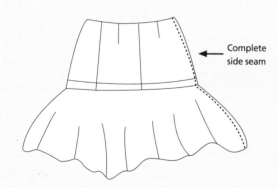

← Complete side seam

10. Stitch Side Seam

Place right sides of skirt together, then stitch the remaining side seam. Press.

11. Turn

Turn right-side out. That's it! Try the skirt on your doll, along with the sweater from page 75.

80

Button-o-Rama!

Buttons! I love them! Buttons offer endless possibilities for practical closures and delicious decorations. My favorite button is the man's dress shirt button; they are plentiful and just the right size for doll clothes. You can get button grab bags at your local quilt shop, fabric store or craft store; they are a great value!

According to Martha Stewart's wonderful website, buttons were once considered jewelry. They were carefully cut from garments and cherished from generation to generation. I love that idea! Buttons really are embellishments, not just fasteners. Here are some of my favorite techniques for embellishing with buttons.

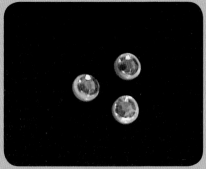

Bejeweled Buttons

Sew on a small shirt button with strong thread, taking just one stitch in each hole so that the surface of the button will remain flat. Put a little fabric glue on a plate. Dip a cotton swab in the glue, then carefully dab a bit of glue in the well of the button. Place a ¼-inch (6mm) flat-backed rhinestone onto the glue with tweezers. Let dry completely.

Stacked Buttons

This is so easy! Just pick two buttons in coordinating colors, then stack them. Make sure the smaller button is on top if you are using two sizes. Stitch the lower button in place first with a doubled length of strong thread. Then, stack the smaller button on top and stitch in place. Flatter buttons work best for this technique.

Buttons and Bows

Thread a wide-eyed embroidery needle with a single strand of lightweight ⅛-inch (3mm) ribbon. Place a two- or four-holed button at the desired spot on the fabric. Insert the needle into one hole from the front, then come back up through the other hole. Remove the needle from the ribbon, tie a bow, and trim the excess ribbon.

Painted Buttons

Can't find buttons in the color you want? Buy white buttons and paint them. Use acrylic paint to make sure the color will stick to the button. Before you paint, thread a wide-eyed embroidery needle with yarn and run the yarn through the button's holes to keep them clear while you paint. Dab the acrylic paint onto the button with a small soft paintbrush. Let dry completely, then pull out the yarn.

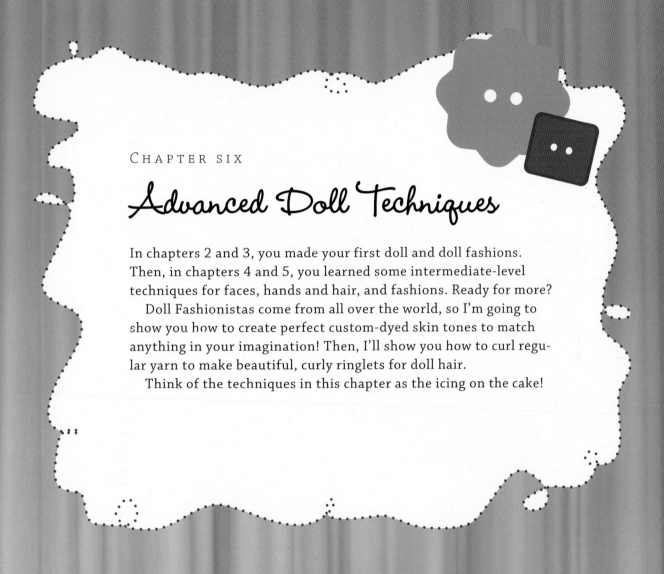

CHAPTER SIX

Advanced Doll Techniques

In chapters 2 and 3, you made your first doll and doll fashions. Then, in chapters 4 and 5, you learned some intermediate-level techniques for faces, hands and hair, and fashions. Ready for more?

Doll Fashionistas come from all over the world, so I'm going to show you how to create perfect custom-dyed skin tones to match anything in your imagination! Then, I'll show you how to curl regular yarn to make beautiful, curly ringlets for doll hair.

Think of the techniques in this chapter as the icing on the cake!

A few months ago, I came across an interesting article that described how the current selection of dolls readily available in the market made some customers uncomfortable because the clothes were too revealing and unappealing. I couldn't help but think that *Doll Fashionistas* could offer a perfect solution to this dilemma! Because we are able to design virtually any type of clothing, we can create fashions that everyone can love. One of my first steps was to purchase a copy of *Muslim Girl* magazine, a wonderful publication that covers many aspects of teenage life including all types of fashion-forward options. For example, the darling outfit shown on the facing page is a very cool long-sleeved top with a modest high neckline, paired with stylish pants. Creating this outfit was a lot of fun. I hope you like it too!

Custom Skin Tones

A wonderful way to create the perfect shade of doll skin is to use some of today's fantastic fabric dyes. These dyes come in bright, vivid colors, and the dyeing process is easy and fun! Clean-up requires only soap and water. The dyes set after air-drying for 24 hours, and the vivid colors stay true after drying.

The best way to create skin tones with fabric dye is to begin with a light-colored felt, then apply color to it.

Dyeing Felt for Custom Skin Tones
Here is a doll on which one arm (the darker one) has been dyed. See the difference? Imagine the infinite skin-tone variations you can create when you are in control of the color mixing! Look on the next page for skin-tone recipes, and experiment to create your own.

WHAT YOU'LL NEED

MATERIALS

- A doll made in light-colored felt, with all parts stuffed and closed but not yet assembled.

- ½ cup (118ml) water (1 cup if you are making a double batch)

- Fabric color in brown, white or ecru (see recipes on facing page), 2-oz. (59ml) jar, Jacquard Dye-na-Flow or any good brand

- Dye-na-Flow Exciter Kit (assorted colors in ½-oz. (15ml) bottles, or assorted colors of any good-quality dye brand

TOOLS

- Two or three 1" (25mm) foam brushes (available at any craft, paint or hardware store)

- Two large plastic garbage bags to protect the work surface

- Duct tape or other strong tape to tape the bags in place

- Inexpensive soft synthetic liner paintbrushes, narrow and pointed, for shading

- 16-oz. (½ liter) jar with screw top (shallow jars are better)

- Ice-cube tray or small containers for mixing dyes

Skin Tone Dye Recipes

Skin is made up of many different colors. While you can purchase a jar of brown or ecru dye, using one color "out of the jar" will give you a flat and uninteresting result. Below are some dye recipes that will bring more subtlety and shading to your doll's skin. We will also use red shades of dye to begin the blushing process on the cheeks, and we'll use blues, browns and grays for shadows in the eye area to create an even more realistic-looking doll.

The following recipes are for one batch. Darker colors require two applications of dye for smooth, even color, so for darker skin tones such as warm brown and pecan brown, double the recipes shown here. Doubling the batch, rather than making two separate batches, will also ensure that the color matches from one application to the next.

To each recipe, add ½ cup water.

Warm Brown: 2 tablespoons Brown + 4 tablespoons Ecru + 1½ teaspoons Pink + 1 teaspoon Gold

Pecan Brown: 1 tablespoon Brown + 4 tablespoons Ecru + 1 tablespoon White + 1 teaspoon Pink + 1 teaspoon Orange + ½ teaspoon Red

Tan: 1 teaspoon Brown + 4 tablespoons Ecru + 1 tablespoon White + 1 teaspoon Pink + 1 teaspoon Red + 1 teaspoon Yellow. (Check color as you go; you may want to add a bit more White.)

Olive: 4 tablespoons Ecru + 2 tablespoons White + 1 teaspoon Gold + 2 teaspoons Pink + ½ teaspoon and a little more Red + 10 drops Green

Golden: 4 tablespoons Ecru + 2 tablespoons White + ¼ teaspoon Brown + 1½ teaspoons Gold + 1 teaspoon Pink + ½ teaspoon Red

Peach: 2 tablespoons Ecru + 4 tablespoons White + ½ teaspoon Orange + ½ teaspoon Gold + 10 drops and a little bit more Brown + 1 teaspoon Pink

Pale Porcelain: 4 tablespoons White + 1½ tablespoon Ecru + 1 teaspoon Pink

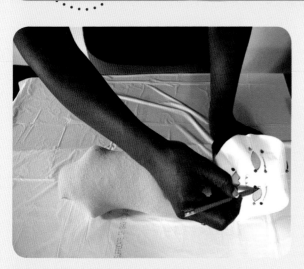

1. Trace the Facial Features Before Dyeing

Using the Face Positioning Template (page 115), pencil in the facial features with a regular no. 2 graphite pencil. The graphite will not smudge during the dyeing process, and you will be able to add blush and shadow to the doll's face more accurately.

2. Prepare Dye and Test the Colors

Choose your skin color recipe from above. Measure the dye colors into a shallow jar with a screw-on lid (the jar should be large enough to hold 1½ cups). Add ½ cup water, screw the lid on tightly, then shake to mix.

To make sure the color is the one you want, brush a little bit onto a scrap of felt, then put the scrap into a 170 degree oven for about ten minutes to dry it. If you like the color, then you're good to go.

Protect Your Workspace

Cover your worktable with plastic to protect it from dye splashes. I like to use a garbage bag secured with duct tape.

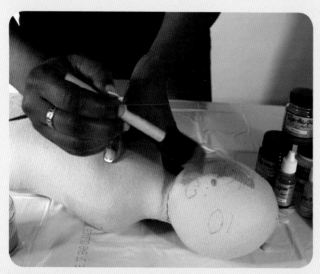

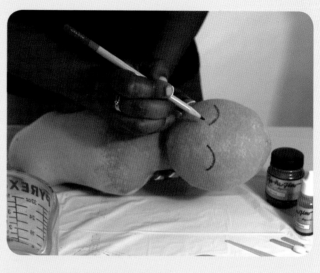

3. Begin Applying Dye to the Face

Dip a clean foam brush into the dye batch. Gently spread the dye on the doll, starting with the head.

4. Line and/or Shade the Eyes

While the face area is still wet, you can line and shade the eyes with watercolor pencils. Of course, make sure to practice on a scrap of felt first.

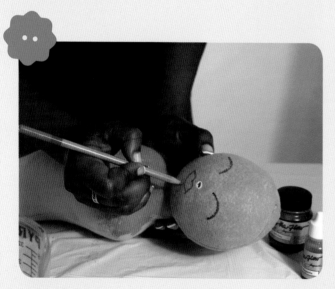

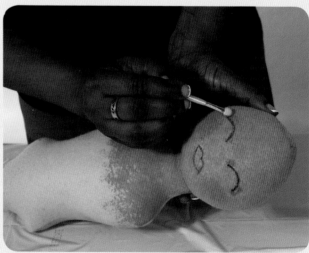

5. Line the Lips

Accentuate the lips with red or red-orange watercolor pencil.

6. Shade Above the Eyelids

Add a few more drops of Brown or Blue to this mixture. Dip a clean foam eye shadow applicator into this new color and lightly and carefully apply a little shadow over the upper eye area, between the eyebrow and the eye.

7. Blush the Cheeks

Mix a few drops of Red (or Red and White) with a few drops of water. Dip a clean foam brush into this mixture and dab lightly on the apples of the cheeks to create a hint of blush.

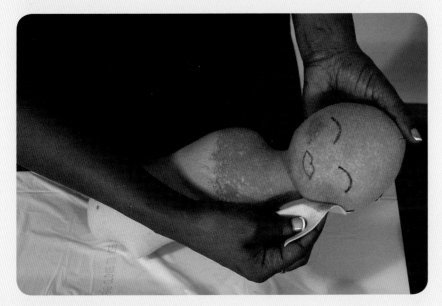

8. Blend and Soften the Cheeks

While the cheek color is still wet, remove excess color and soften the edges with a scrap of felt.

9. Dye the Rest of the Doll

Apply dye to the rest of the doll. Make sure to cover her completely; check between the fingers, under the sculpting threads of the toes, and at the fronts and backs of the knees, where there tend to be creases. Work quickly to make sure that the doll is covered evenly with dye and that spots do not form. Let the color dry completely, then evaluate the evenness of the color. If any areas are uneven, spritz lightly with a fine water mist and re-apply some more color.

10. Shade the Knee Sockets

Put a small amount of the dye recipe in an ice cube tray or other small container. Add two or three drops of Dark Brown and a drop or two of Pink to create a slightly deeper shade of the dye. Dilute this mixture with a few drops of water. If the dye is dry, spritz the knees lightly with a fine water mist; then, using a pointed soft synthetic paintbrush, apply a little of this shadow mixture to the knee socket.

11. Let Dry, Then Paint the Face

Set the doll aside to air-dry for 24 hours. A faster alternative is to set your oven to 170° F (11° C) and put the doll face up on a piece of foil in the oven for 90 minutes. Once the doll is dry, you can proceed with painting the face, starting on page 90.

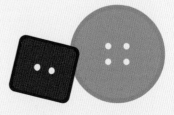

Making Curly Hair

What about curly heads? It's fun and easy to make curly doll hair, from loose silky curls to tight, flirty, kinky curls. The choice is yours!

WHAT YOU'LL NEED

MATERIALS

- Yarn (one skein of 50 yards or more will be more than enough for one head of curly hair)

TOOLS

- Soft cotton towel
- Oven
- Metal knitting needles in the diameter of the curls you want

Experiment!

Try different sizes of knitting needles for curls. Fatter needles will make looser curls; skinnier ones will make tighter curls. You might even try curling some unconventional materials, such as ribbon, to see what happens!

Make Your Own Curly Yarn for Doll Hair

All you need to curl yarn for doll hair are some metal knitting needles and water. It's pretty much like setting straight hair on curlers.

At a salon, the setting process is accelerated with warm air dryers. To speed the drying time for yarn, you can use a slow oven. Just be sure to use only metal needles. You can air-dry the curls with equal success; it will just take longer (three to four hours on a warm day).

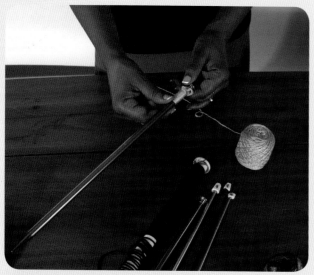 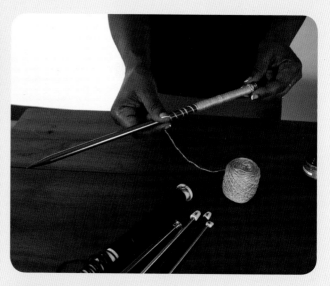

1. Preheat and Prepare

Preheat your oven to 170°F (11°C) .

Attach the yarn at the base of a metal knitting needle using a slipknot.

2. Wind, Wet and Set

Wind the yarn tightly in a single layer around the knitting needle. When you get near the end of the needle, cut the yarn and secure the loose end by tying it down with a short length of yarn.

Wet the yarn-wrapped needles with cool water. Blot out excess water with a soft towel.

Place the yarn-wrapped metal knitting needles in the preheated 170°F (11°C) oven, directly on the rack to maximize air circulation. After about 90 minutes, remove the needles from the oven. Let them cool a few minutes, then feel the yarn to make sure it's completely dry.

3. Make Wefts With the Hair Loom

(facing page)

Unwind the now-curly yarn from the knitting needle. Wind the curled yarn onto the Hair Loom as directed on page 37, except you'll want to wind it more loosely than you would with uncurled yarn. Then stitch down the center just as directed on page 37. Hand-stitch the wefts of curls onto the doll's head, then shake to bring out the curls.

About the Yarn

For this demonstration, I used a South African yarn in a sun-drenched gold color. This yarn is made from bamboo! It has a beautiful sheen and subtle variegation because it is hand-dyed. I curled the yarn on a no. 19 knitting needle for this doll; you can see the result on the facing page.

Curly Hair Variations

The size of the knitting needle changes the look, but so does the way you attach the wefts. As explained on page 66, you can attach all the wefts horizontally for a short-haired look, or you can attach some vertically for a longer style. These are just some of the possibilities for curled hair!

Medium Curls, Attached Vertically

Loose Curls, Attached Vertically

Medium Curls (Bangs Only), Attached Horizontally

Tight Curls, Attached Vertically

CHAPTER SEVEN

Advanced Fashion Techniques

Re-fashion, deconstruct and reconstruct!! Buy retail and add your own detail! This fun process can be as easy and simple or as detailed and challenging as you want. Best of all, all of the techniques can be used on full-sized ready-to-wear clothes, too. You could even create matching Fashionista outfits for you and your doll!

Also in this chapter, you will learn an exciting heirloom sewing technique inspired by Dr. Martha Pullen, the accomplished sewing innovator on *Martha's Sewing Room*. I've used the same technique with organic linen and laces to create the dress on the facing page.

This doll's outfit reflects an appreciation for our environment. We have only one earth; we should do what ever we can to protect it. Did you know that many fabric companies now manufacture beautiful lines of organic fabrics and trims? The fabrics are woven from organic cottons and colored with pure vegetable dyes. You can find these products at fine quilt shops or online. There are even environmentally friendly fiberfill stuffing products made from corn, and yarns made in a sustainable fashion from bamboo that has been tinted with natural dyes! When these products are combined with antique laces, recycled from garage-sale linens, the result is an eco-conscious Doll Fashionista!

The dress is made with organic linen all in the same color family with lace trim and an entre-deux application of antique organic lace. Her hair is an organic hemp yarn.

Embellished Bear Sweater

You can embellish a ready-to-wear bear sweater to create a trend-setting doll sweater full of fashion fabulosity!

To make doll clothing from retail ready-to-wear, visit the teddy bear aisle at your favorite craft or toy store. Think of these bear clothes as your blank canvases. The sweaters provide you with a perfect size knit stitch, sleeves already set in, and neck and hemlines already finished. All you have to do is embellish.

My goal in making this sweater was to use many embellishments together with the existing knit texture to create a real show-stopper of a sweater. Flowers are my theme.

WHAT YOU'LL NEED
MATERIALS

- One teddy bear sweater for a 20-inch (51cm) bear
- Several colors of narrow silk ribbon or embroidery floss
- Flat-backed rhinestones
- Beads
- Sequins
- 12" (30cm) hook-and-eye tape
- A piece of Steam-A-Seam 2 measuring 6" × 6" (15cm × 15cm)
- A scrap of quilting-weight cotton fabric, 5" × 8" (13cm × 20cm)

TOOLS

- Embroidery needle (with a large eye for floss)
- Sewing scissors
- Iron

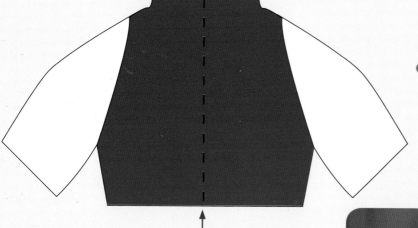

Cutting
Line

1. Create a Center Opening

Don't cut the sweater yet! First, cut a 2" × 6" (5cm × 15cm) piece of Steam-A-Seam 2 to match the shape of the sweater front. Place it on the wrong side of the sweater and iron in place. This will prevent the knit from unraveling when you cut it.

Now, cut the sweater straight down the center front. Just eyeball it.

2. Embroider Some Flowers

Using variegated embroidery floss and an embroidery needle, make several flowers using the *lazy daisy stitch* (see appendix F, page 125). Leave a wide opening in the middle for a rhinestone center. Use green variegated floss to make stems and leaves for the flowers. Use the Bejeweled Button technique (see page 81) for the flower centers.

Front-Opening Sweaters Are Easier to Embellish

Adding a front opening to a sweater gives you a lot of flexibility when embellishing. Because you will not have to pull the sweater over the doll's head, the neckline does not need to stretch, so you can add embellishment with total abandon.

3. Add Closure and Lining

First, we will attach the hook-and-eye tape to the front of the sweater. Cut two pieces of Steam-A-Seam 2 that are ¼-inch (6mm) wide and the length of the sweater opening. Peel the paper backing from the Steam-A-Seam 2, then iron it onto each side of the sweater opening with the right side out. Cut hook-and-eye tape the length of the sweater opening plus ½" (12mm) extra for the top and ½" (12mm) extra for the bottom. Iron the hook-and-eye tape onto the sweater. Remove the remaining paper from the Steam-A-Seam 2. Turn the excess hook-and-eye tape under at the top and bottom, then tack the ends in place on the wrong side with a few hand stitches.

For the lining, cut two pieces of quilting-weight cotton fabric to match the shapes of the sweater fronts, then press a narrow hem on all edges. Peel the paper backing from the Steam-A-Seam 2 and iron it to the wrong side of the sweater fronts.

Voilà! Your doll has a one-of-a-kind topper to pair with jeans or a simple jean skirt.

Heirloom Dress

This dress looks difficult, but is very simple to make (easy peasy!). It's based on our basic signature sundress from chapter three. The "heirloom" features include insertion lace, entre-deux (pronounced an-tray-doe) techniques and bridal button-loop closures. I learned the entre-deux technique watching *Martha's Sewing Room* on PBS . . . thank you, Dr. Martha Pullen! And I learned the bridal button loop technique from watching Nancy Zieman, with whom I had the extraordinary privilege and pleasure of making the DVD that accompanies this book. Nancy's guest, Mary Mulari, made button loops using colorful elastic hair bands!

WHAT YOU'LL NEED

MATERIALS

- ¼ yard or meter of light weight woven white fabric
- ⅝" (17mm) lace with a straight finish on both edges, 2 yards or meters
- Contrasting ½ inch (12mm) ribbon for insertion, 1 yard or meter
- 1" (25mm) flat lace with a straight finish on both edges, 1 yard or meter
- 1" (25mm) flat lace with one straight edge and one decorative edge, 1 yard or meter
- 12 small buttons, about ¼" (6mm) diameter
- White satin cord, 1 yard or meter

TOOLS

- Large safety pin

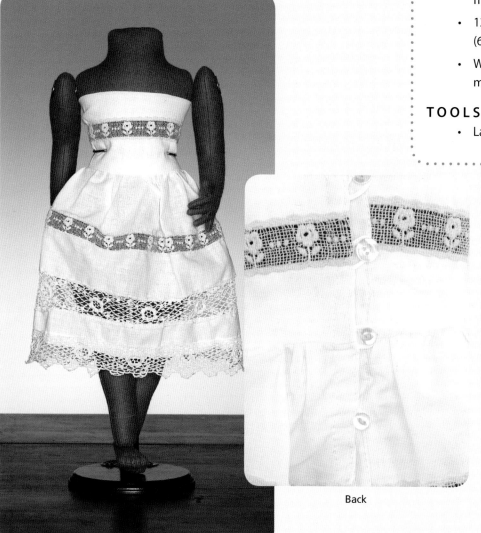

Back

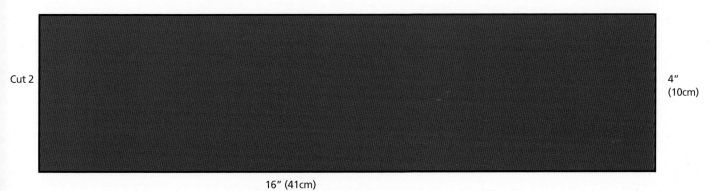

Cut 2

4"
(10cm)

16" (41cm)

1. Cut Bodice Pieces

Cut two rectangles measuring 4" × 16" (10cm × 41cm) for the bodice.

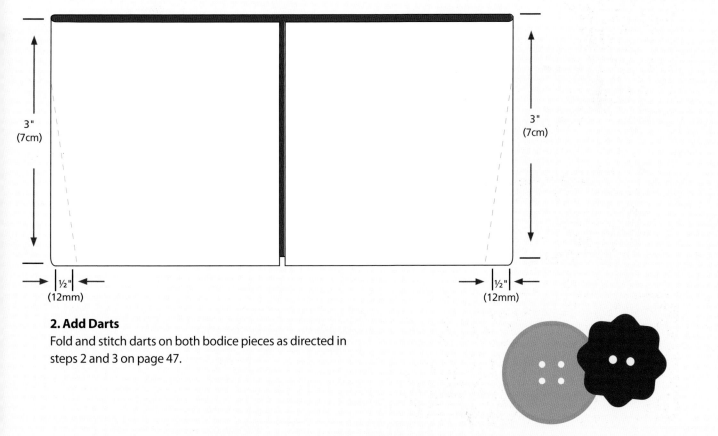

3"
(7cm)

3"
(7cm)

½"
(12mm)

½"
(12mm)

2. Add Darts

Fold and stitch darts on both bodice pieces as directed in steps 2 and 3 on page 47.

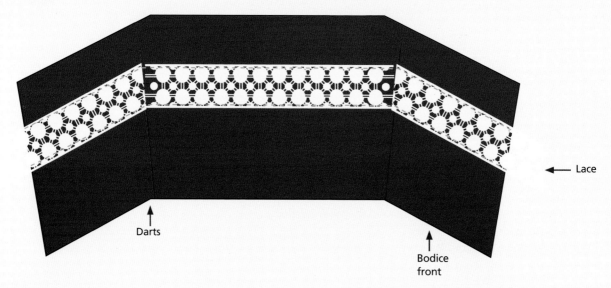

Lace

Darts

Bodice
front

3. Add Insertion Lace

Take one of the bodice pieces and place the insertion lace on the bodice with its top edge 2 inches (5cm) down from the top edge of the bodice piece. Using a normal stitch length of 10 stitches per inch, stitch along both edges of the lace, close to the edges.

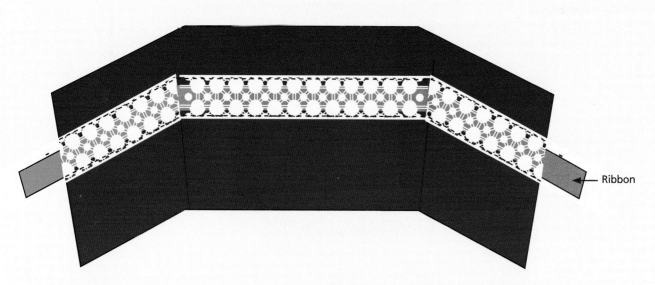

Ribbon

4. Insert Ribbon

Attach a large safety pin to one end of the ribbon, then use the pin to insert the ribbon between the lace and the bodice. Pull the ribbon all the way through the lace channel. Baste the ribbon in place at both ends, then clip off excess ribbon and lace.

Complete the bodice following steps 6 and 7 on pages 48–49.

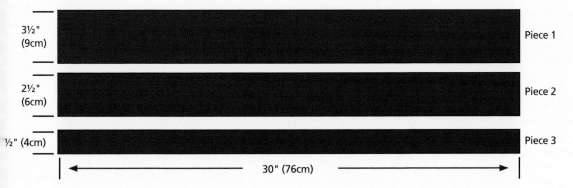

3½"
(9cm)
Piece 1

2½"
(6cm)
Piece 2

½" (4cm)
Piece 3

30" (76cm)

5. Cut the Skirt Pieces

For the skirt pieces, cut three rectangles of fabric in the following sizes:

Piece 1: 3½" × 30" (9cm × 76cm)
Piece 2: 2½" × 30" (6cm × 76cm)
Piece 3: 1½" × 30" (4cm × 76cm)

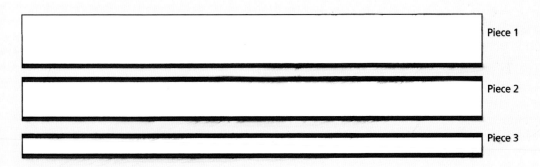

Piece 1

Piece 2

Piece 3

6. Press Under the Edges

Press under ¼" (6mm) on the long edges of all three skirt pieces except for the top edge of piece 1, which will be gathered later.

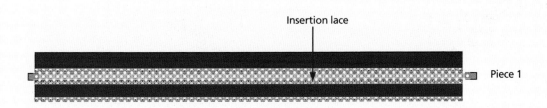

Insertion lace

Piece 1

7. Stitch Lace to Piece 1

Add insertion lace and ribbon to center of piece 1 using the same process as in steps 2 and 3.

Overlap a piece of lace slightly with the bottom edge of Piece 1 (both pieces with their right sides facing up) and machine-stitch where they overlap with either a straight stitch or a very narrow zigzag stitch. This is the entre-deux technique.

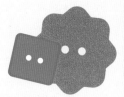

Piece 1

Piece 2

8. Attach Skirt Piece 2

Stitch Piece 2 to the other edge of the lace in the same manner as step 7.

Stitch a second piece of the lace with two straight edges to the bottom edge of Piece 2.

Piece 1

Piece 2

Piece 3

9. Attach Skirt Piece 3

Stitch Piece 3 to the remaining edge of the lace.

Finally, stitch the lace with one decorative edge to the other side of Piece 3 with the decorative side at the hemline.

Add insertion lace and ribbon to the center of Piece 3 using the same process as in steps 2 and 3.

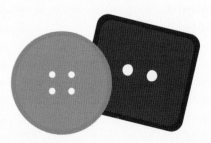

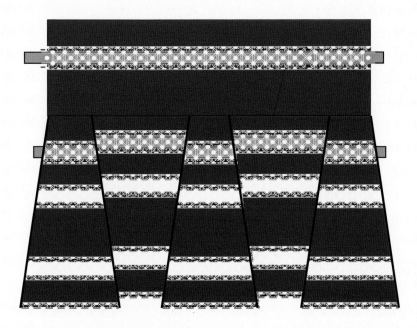

10. Gather and Attach the Skirt

Follow steps 12–15 on pages 50–51 to gather the skirt and attach it to the bodice.

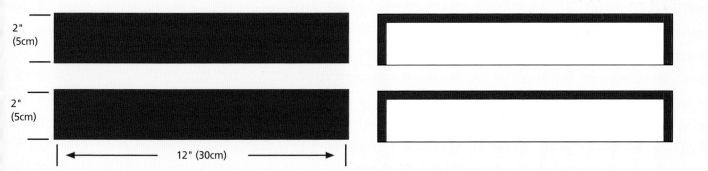

2"
(5cm)

2"
(5cm)

12" (30cm)

11. Cut Back Facings

For the back facings, cut two strips of fabric, each measuring 2" × 12" (5cm × 30cm).

12. Press Back Facings

Press under ¼" (6mm) on three sides of each strip as shown.

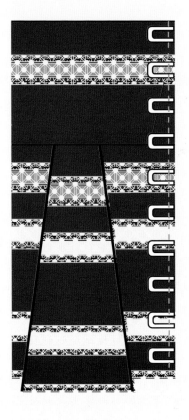
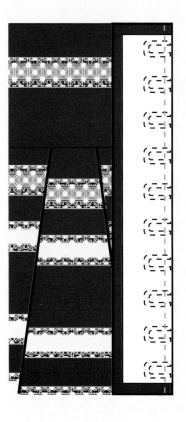
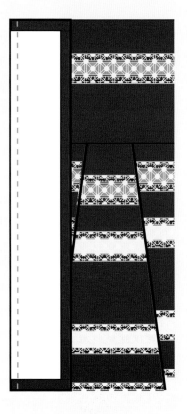

13. Make Bridal Button Loops

Cut ten pieces of satin cord, each 2"
(5cm) long.

Baste loops in place on the right
side of the fabric ⅛inch (3mm) from
edge, raw ends flush with the raw
edge of the dress back as shown.

14. Stitch First Back Facing

Place one facing strip right side down
on top of the button loops, matching the unpressed raw edge with the
raw edge of the dress back. Pin in
place. Stitch the raw edges together
with a standard ¼-inch (6mm) seam
allowance. This will secure the loops in
place as well as attaching the facing.

15. Stitch Second Facing

Attach the other facing strip to the
other side of the dress back in the
same manner as in step 14.

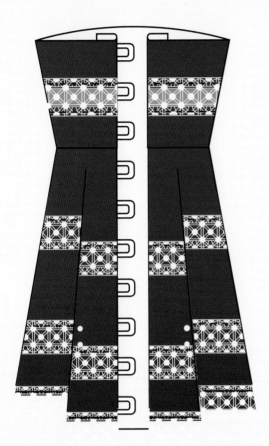

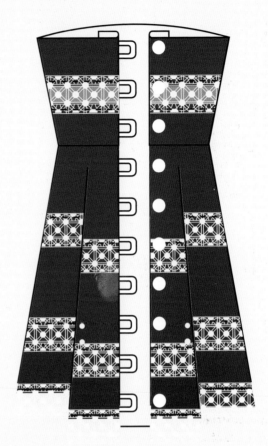

16. Press Back Edges Under

Press both back edges under along the seams you stitched in the previous step.

17. Add Buttons

Using extra-strong thread, sew the buttons to the dress back, opposite from the button loops.

That's it! You've created a beautiful heirloom-style dress for your doll.

You could also make a funky version of this dress just by changing fabric color(s), trims and buttons!

Fashionista Trousers

How about a perfect pair of pants? You can embellish these easy trousers to your heart's content because there are only two simple seams. Remember, it is easiest to embellish while the pattern pieces are still flat, before you stitch any seams.

Fashionista Trousers
You can make these trousers using denim or any other fabric. The pants will fit best if the fabric contains lycra or something to give it a bit of stretch. Stretch denim would be great for a casual look; stretch velour would create a dressy look. Check out these funky fatigues, made from cotton knit!

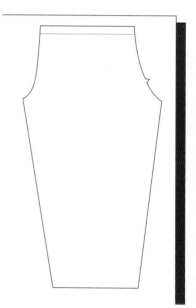

1. Cut the Pattern Pieces
Fold your fabric in half with right sides facing. Lay the trouser pattern on the folded fabric, trace and cut to get two trouser legs.

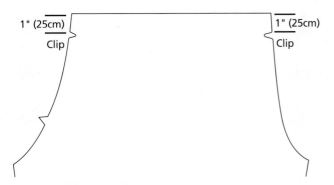

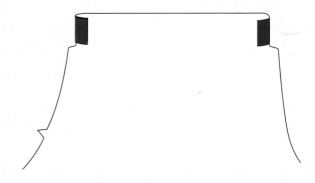

2 .Make Two Small Clips

Make two small clips on each trouser piece, 1 inch (25mm) from the top edge, as shown.

1" (25cm)
Clip

1" (25cm)
Clip

3 .Press Hem for Ribbon Casing

Fold the fabric inward above the clips you made in step 2; press. This will make finished openings for the ribbon casing.

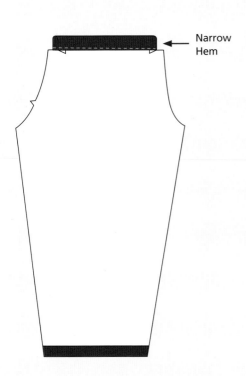

Narrow Hem

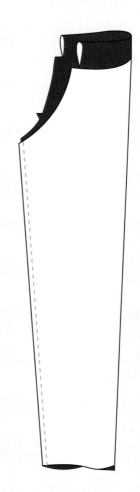

4 .Turn Hems and Ribbon Casing

Turn and stitch a ¼-inch (6mm) hem at the waist. Do the same for each pant cuff if desired (you may prefer a raw edge finish, it's up to you!).

Now is the time to embellish the pants if you wish. Be sure to leave room for a ¼ inch (6mm) seam allowance on both sides and a ½ inch (12mm) seam allowance at the waist.

Turn under another ½ inch (12mm) at the waist to create a casing for the ribbon. Press. Sew the casing in place ³⁄8 inch (10mm) from the top edge of the pants.

5. Stitch the Inside Seams

Fold one leg piece right-sides together and stitch the inside seam, as shown. Repeat for the other leg.

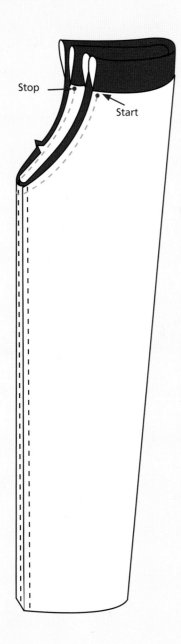

6. Stitch the Crotch Seam

This step is a little tricky; just follow along and take your time:

Turn one pant leg right side out. Slip that leg into the other pant leg so that the right sides are together. Match the notches and you'll know that you are on the right track.

Stitch the crotch seam, starting at the notch and stopping ½ inch (12mm) from the bottom edge of the casing.

7. Insert Ribbon Waist Tie

Turn the pants right-side out. Attach a safety pin to one end of the ribbon. Run the ribbon through the waist casing. The ribbon will peek through in the back where the casing seams meet.

That's it! Try the pants on your doll. Draw up the ribbon and tie a beautiful bow.

Distressed Jeans!

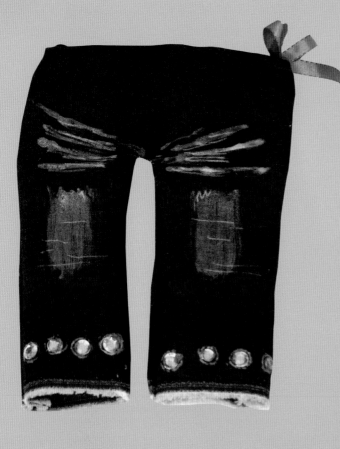

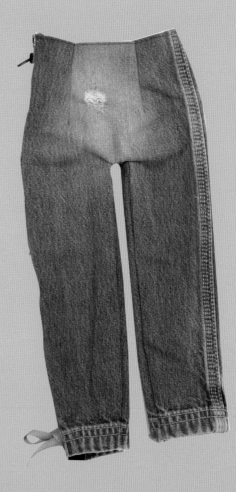

Distress the Fabric With a Bleach Pen!

For a unique and up-to-date touch, make the fashionista trousers in dark indigo denim and then "distress" the fabric. Insert a piece of cardboard in each jean leg (this is to keep the bleach pen from bleeding through). Using a very light touch, delicately draw three to five straight horizontal lines on each leg as shown. Dry the jeans in the sun for about one hour. The bleach pen will turn white and cakey. Use a wet paper towel to wipe away the dried bleach, then let the pants air-dry. Embellish if desired!

Recycle Distressed Jeans

This version was created with fabric from a worn pair of jeans. You can create a hole by sanding an already-thin area with sandpaper. Notice that we have used the original side seam and hems to give an authentic, well-worn and well-loved jeans feeling.

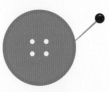

Conclusion

Well, that's it! By completing this book, you have learned most of the sewing techniques you would cover in a Sewing 101 course. If you'd like more, visit us at www.TheDollLoft.com, where we carry all of the materials and supplies mentioned in this book. You will also find the hottest patterns for the fashions featured on the runway, new dolls and new doll accessories (hats, scarves, handbags, etc.)!

We hope you've enjoyed *Doll Fashionistas*! I loved writing this for you!

All the best,
Ellen Lumpkin Brown

Appendix A: Patterns for Doll Body

Quick Reference:

How to Use the Doll Body Patterns

Chapter 2 explains how to use the doll body pattern pieces. The process is different for doll bodies than for garments, so be sure to follow the steps in chapter 2.

Once you've learned the process, you can flip to this "Quick Reference" anytime you need a refresher.

1. Photocopy the pattern pieces at 100% size from this appendix, unless otherwise indicated on the pattern.
2. Cut out the paper pattern pieces.
3. Fold the felt in half and position pattern pieces on it. (Remember, felt has no right side and no bias, so you can position the pieces any direction.)
4. Trace the pattern pieces onto the felt.
5. Transfer pattern markings onto the felt (reference points, darts, and turning openings).
6. Stitch on the traced lines, except do not stitch openings, and do not stitch lines that are marked on the pattern pieces as cutting lines.
7. Cut around the sewn parts, cutting $1/8$ inch (3mm) from stitching and ¼ inch (6mm) from openings.
8. For pattern pieces marked "cutting line," cut them out along the traced lines.

Make Your Own Reusable Templates!

To make durable, reusable pattern pieces onto lightweight cardboard. Be sure to also transfer the markings that show where to leave openings for turning.

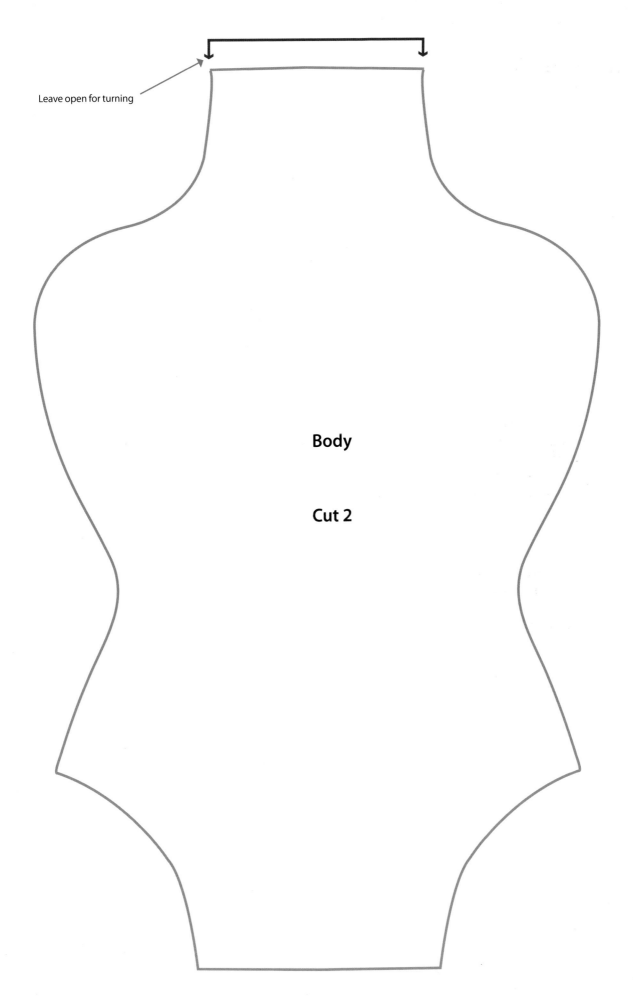

Leave open for turning

Body

Cut 2

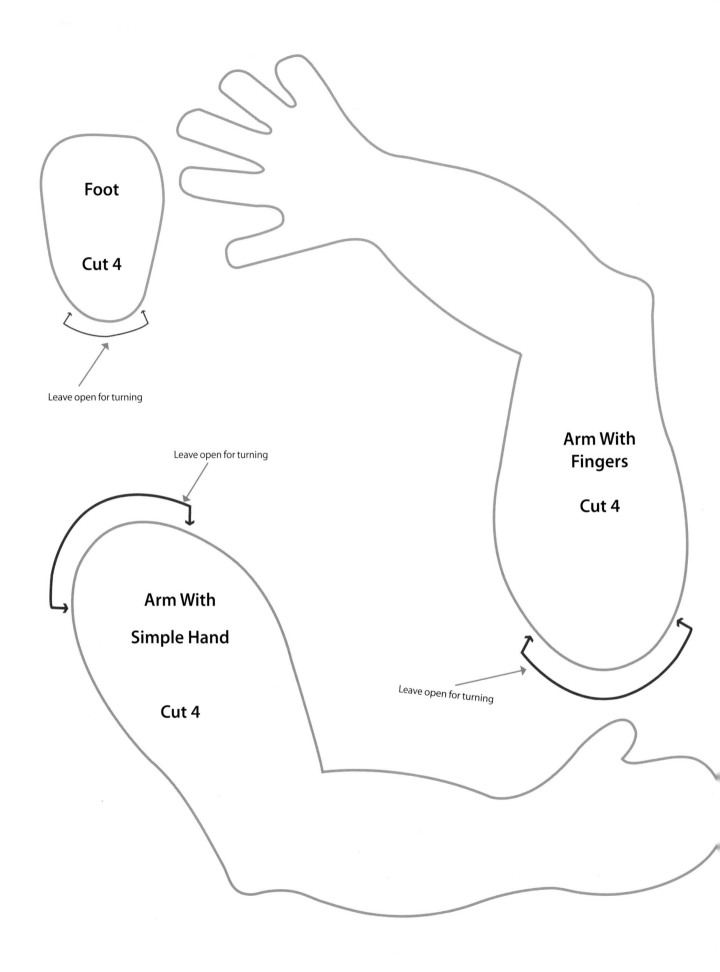

Foot

Cut 4

Leave open for turning

Leave open for turning

Arm With
Fingers

Cut 4

Leave open for turning

Arm With

Simple Hand

Cut 4

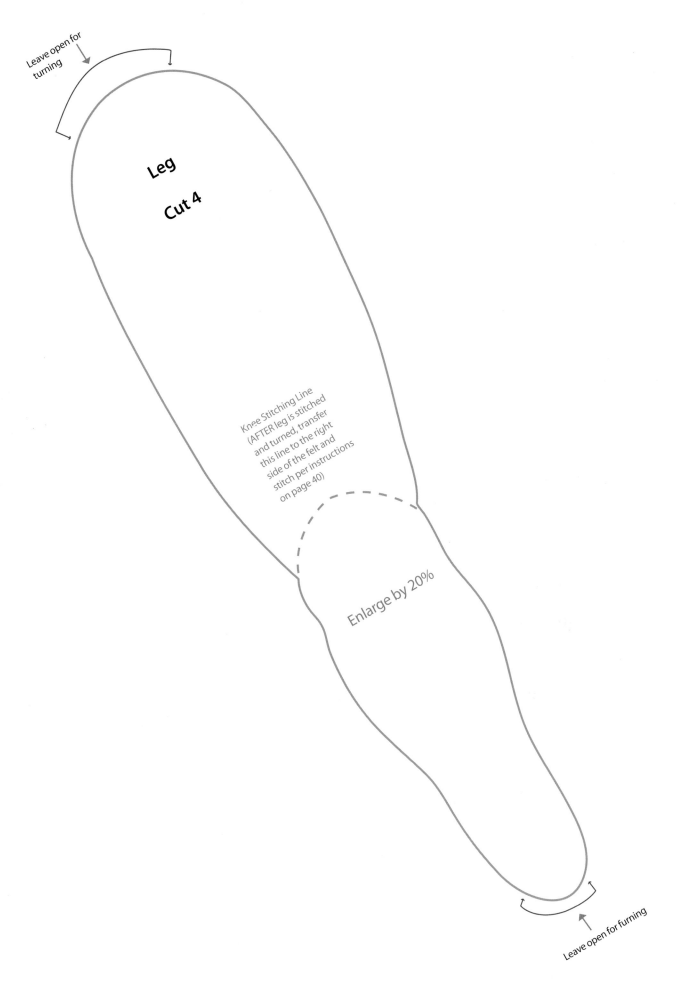

Leave open for turning

Leave open for turning

Leave open for turning

Leg

Cut 4

Knee Stitching Line (AFTER leg is stitched and turned, transfer this line to the right side of the felt and stitch per instructions on page 40)

Enlarge by 20%

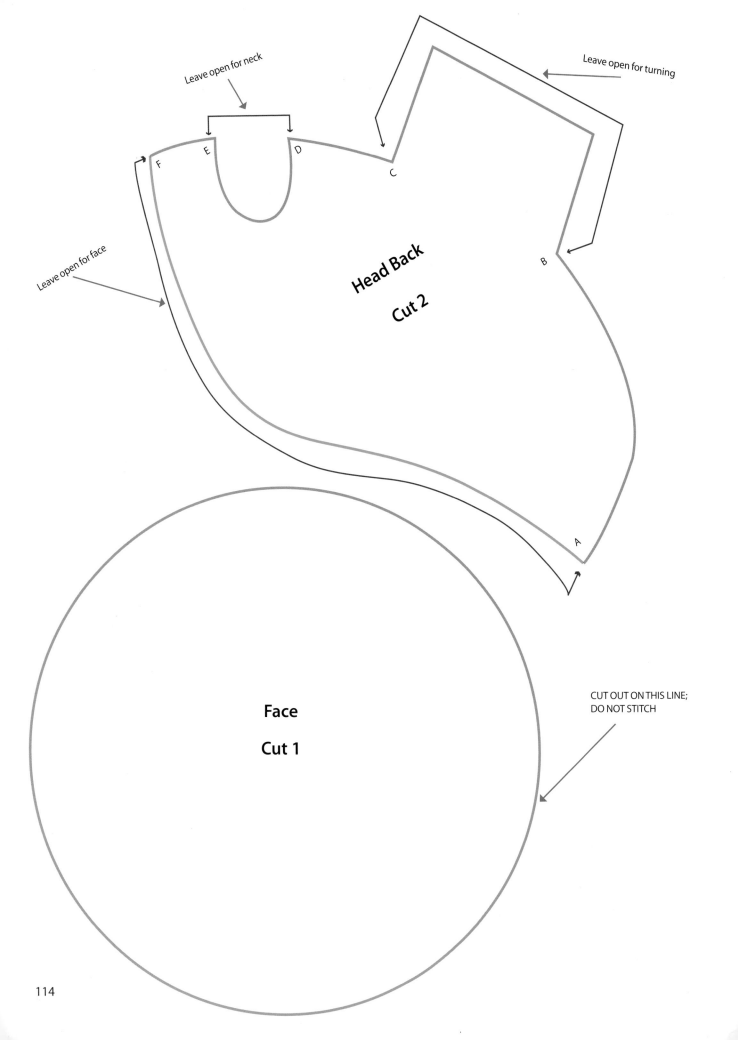

Leave open for neck

Leave open for turning

Leave open for face

E

F

D

C

B

A

Head Back

Cut 2

Face

Cut 1

CUT OUT ON THIS LINE;
DO NOT STITCH

Appendix B: Face and Hair Templates

FACE POSITIONING TEMPLATE

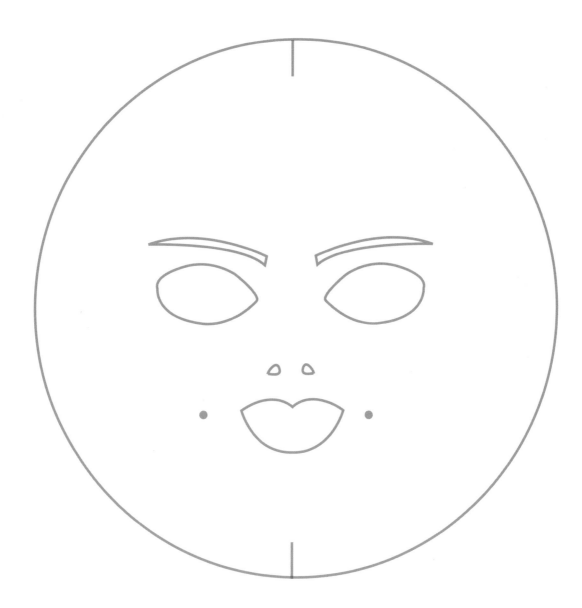

Hair Loom

(centimeters)   (inches)

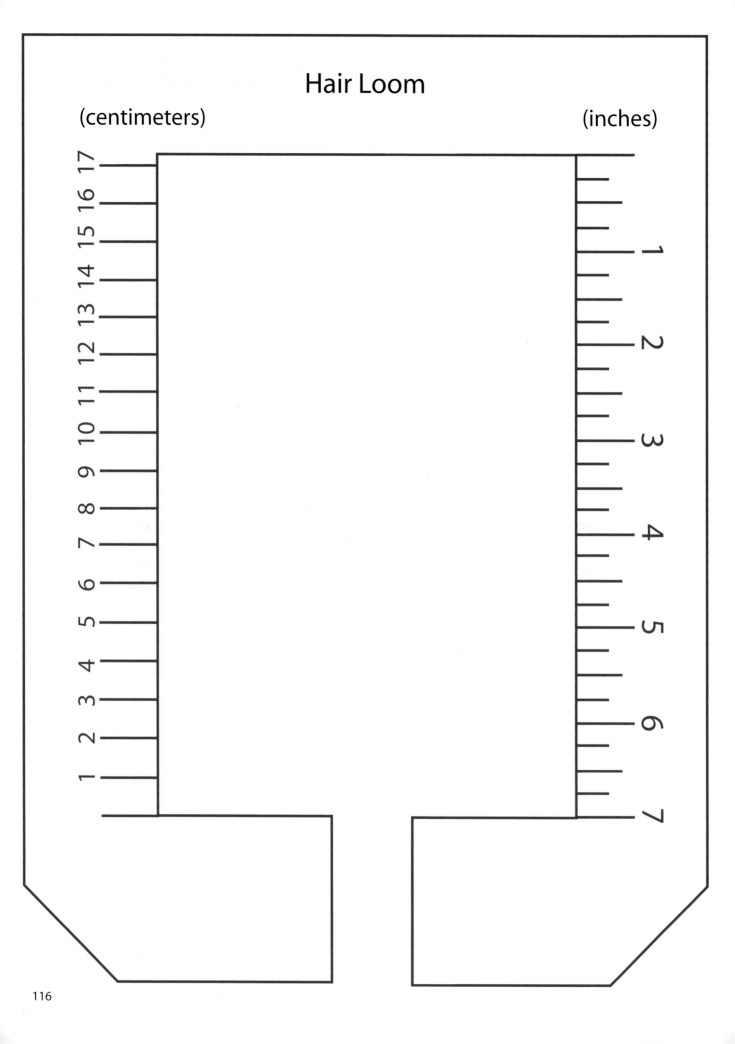

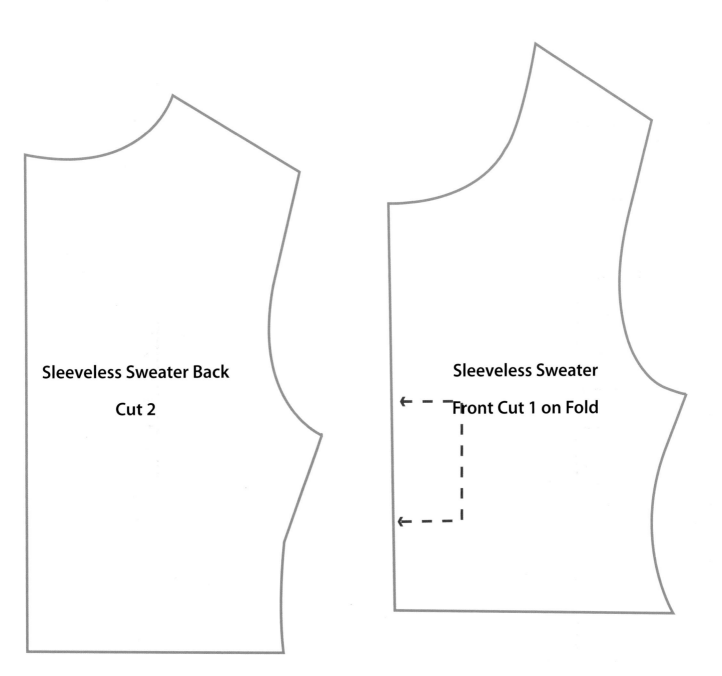

Sleeveless Sweater Back

Cut 2

Sleeveless Sweater

Front Cut 1 on Fold

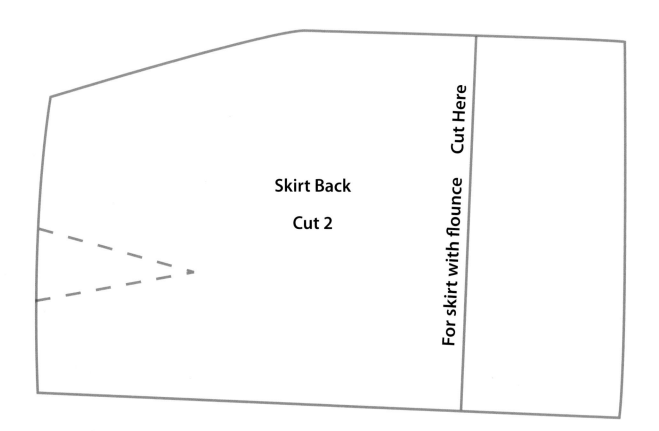

Skirt Back

Cut 2

For skirt with flounce   Cut Here

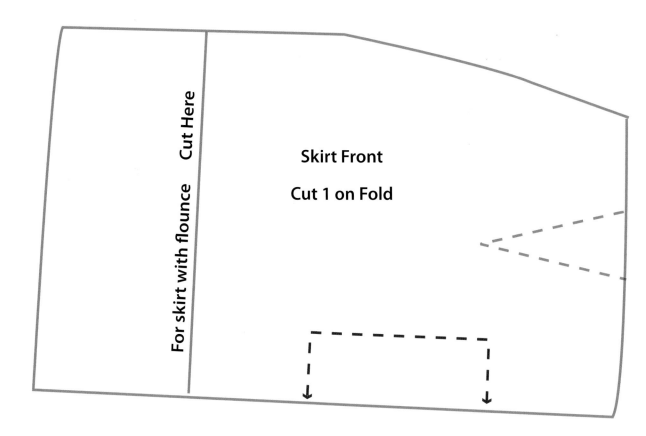

For skirt with flounce   Cut Here

Skirt Front

Cut 1 on Fold

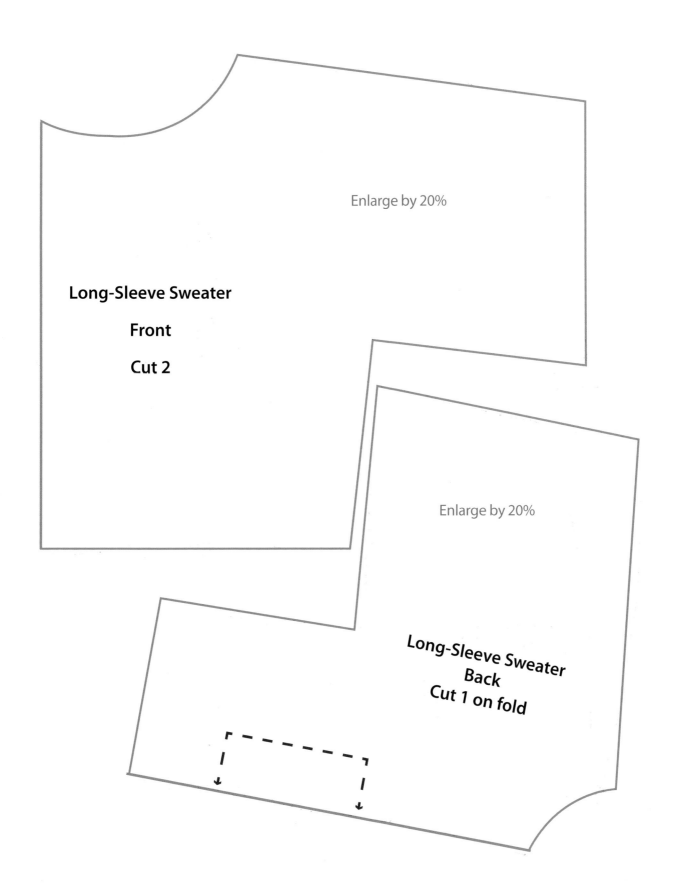

Long-Sleeve Sweater

Front

Cut 2

Enlarge by 20%

Long-Sleeve Sweater
Back
Cut 1 on fold

Enlarge by 20%

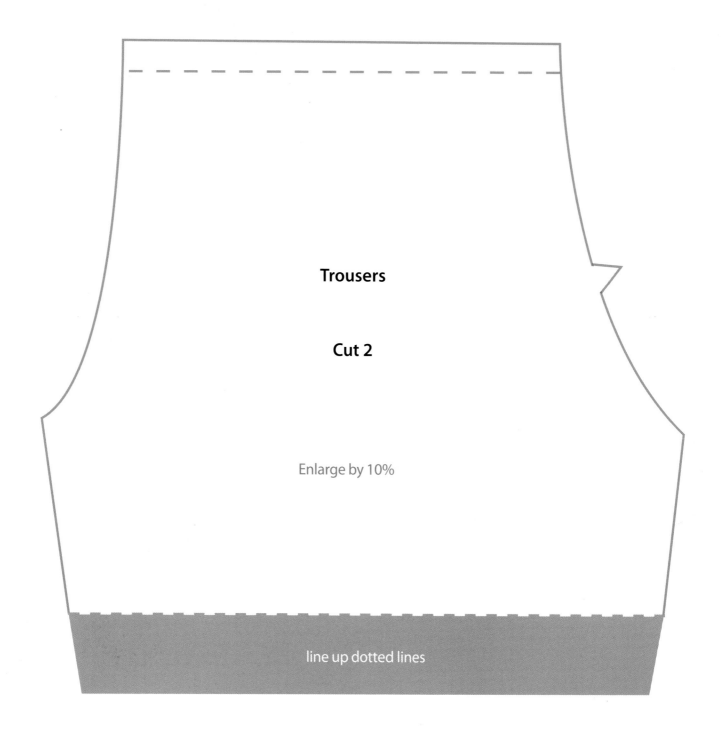

Trousers

Cut 2

Enlarge by 10%

line up dotted lines

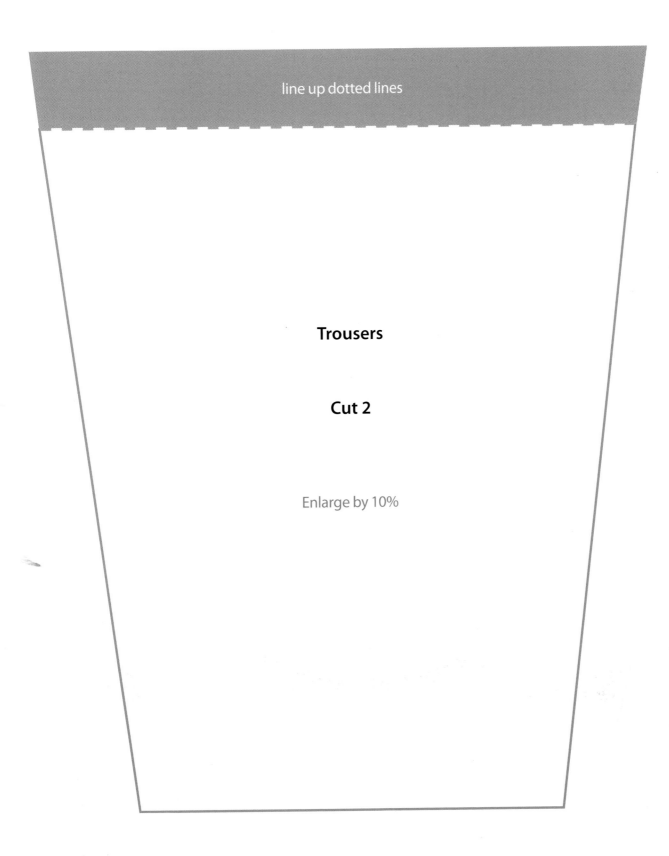

line up dotted lines

Trousers

Cut 2

Enlarge by 10%

Appendix D: Resources

THE DOLL LOFT
Our website featuring everything needed to create Doll Fashionistas and stunning doll fashions. Please visit us often. We believe in fast fashion and we are always creating new doll patterns and doll fashion patterns.
www.TheDollLoft.com

MORE DOLL MAKERS' SITES
Patti Culea's Designs
Incredible dolls, books and patterns. Patti's books are excellent for learning doll making, creating doll faces, doll clothes and art techniques.
www.PMCdesigns.com

Mimi Winer
Patterns and tutorials
www.mimidolls.com

Barbara Willis Designs
Doll-making patterns
www.barbarawillisdesigns.com

Doll Street Dreamers
Community, patterns, challenges
www.DollStreetDreamers.com

DOLL MAKING SUPPLIES
Sisters and Daughters
Patterns and supplies
www.SistersandDaughters.com

Edinburgh Imports
A wonderful, wonderful source for 100 percent wool felt (a wide variety of colors) and other hard to find notions. Their main business is Teddy Bear making.
www.EdinburghImports.com

Doll Maker's Journey
Patterns, supplies and great newsletter
www.DollMakersJourney.com

Joggles
All kinds of hard to find doll making supplies
www.joggles.com

Cloth Doll Connection
Supplies especially for cloth doll makers; Fabulous links to doll makers worldwide
www.ClothDollConnection.com

Lisa's Heaven
Supplies, finished dolls, books and patterns including Australian doll making publications
www.DollHeaven.com

Anita's Doll Supply
U.K. supplier of doll making notions
www.DollSupply.com

Anne's Glory Box
Australian supplier of doll making notions
www.AnnesGloryBox.com.au

PUBLICATIONS
Soft Dolls and Animals Magazine
One of the best cloth doll-making magazines around with lots of patterns, projects and tips.
http://scottpublications.com/sdamag

Art Doll Quarterly
Creative techniques to make dolls of all mediums
www.ArtDollQuarterly.com

Haute Doll Magazine
The magazine for dolls who love to shop! Great fashion inspirations and sometimes free patterns!
www.HauteDoll.com

Doll Crafter and Costuming
Techniques to make and dress all kinds of dolls including patterns, instructions and fashion patterns.
www.dollccmag.com

DOLLS Magazine
All the latest from the doll world
www.DollsMagazine.com

Sew Beautiful Magazine
Lovely heirloom sewing techniques made easy! Martha Pullen is a great resource.
www.SewBeautiful.com

Threads Magazine
The magazine for sewing
www.taunton.com/threads

Be Sew Stylish
A terrific new publication for all kinds of sewing
www.BeSewStylish.com

INSPIRATION
Quilter's TV
A 24/7 web resource with videos and blogs about quilting, doll making and other topics
www.QuiltersTV.com

Sew On TV
A 24/7 web resource with videos and blogs about fashion sewing, quilting, doll making and more
www.SewOnTV.com

America Sews

Exciting sewing techniques that can be applied to dolls and doll fashions
www.AmericaSews.com

Nancy Zieman Productions

The woman who taught us all to sew.
www.nancysnotions.com

Mary Mulari

Great techniques for finishing and embellishing garments that can be applied to doll fashions.
www.marymurlari.com

Needle n Thread

This is an awesome website for hand embroidery instruction!! It includes great information, diagrams to guide you and excellent video tutorials on many embroidery stitches.
www.needlenthread.com

Quilt Central

Techniques from the quilting world
www.QuiltCentral.com

Martha Stewart Living

Videos and instruction sheets for extraordinary sewing projects
www.MarthaStewart.com

House and Garden Television

Videos and projects with crafting diva Carol Duvall
www.HGTV.com

MyCraftivity

All types of crafting inspiration
www.mycraftivity.com

Craft Stylish

More crafting inspiration
www.CraftStylish.com

OTHER SUPPLIERS

Magic Cabin Dolls

Finished dolls and doll-making supplies
www.MagicCabinDolls.com

Prym Dritz

Doll making needles and other notions
www.Dritz.com

Airtex Stuffing

My favorite brand of stuffing for doll making
www.Airtex.com

Near Sea Naturals

A wonderful web store for organic fabrics, laces and notions
www.NearSeaNaturals.com

Prisma Color Pencils

Colored pencils
www.PrismaColor.com

Dye-na-Flow Dyes

Beautiful fabric dyes perfect for dyeing doll skin.
www.Jacquardproducts.com

Caravan Beads

All kinds of beautiful beads
www.CaravanBeads.com

SUPPLIES FOR ALL YOUR

CREATIVE NEEDS

Jo-Ann Fabrics and Crafts

Everything including a great selection of fabrics and notions! Don't forget the upholstery section has cool and unusual fabric options for doll clothes!
www.JoAnn.com

A.C. Moore

Many notions, yarn and doll accessories. A great place for ribbon and for teddy bear sweaters.
www.ACMoore.com

Michaels

Sewing notions, stuffing and plastic pellets and other crafting items.
www.Michaels.com

Appendix E: Machine Stitches

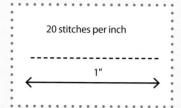

20 stitches per inch

1"

Standard Stitch Length for Felt Doll Bodies

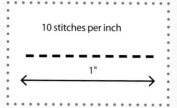

10 stitches per inch

1"

Standard Stitch Length for Doll Garments

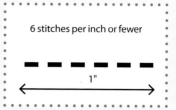

6 stitches per inch or fewer

1"

Stitch Length for Basting or Gathering

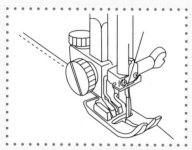

Edge Stitch

A straight stitch done about ⅛" from the edge of the fabric. This stitch can be used on raw or finished edges and with single or double layers of fabric.

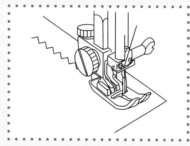

Zigzag Stitch

This W-shaped stitch has many uses: finishing seams, attatching garment pieces and decoration. With a very short stitch length, the zigzag forms a buttonhole or satin stitch.

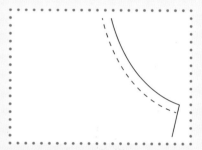

Stay Stitch

Stitching through one layer of fabric to stabilize the fabric. In most cases, stay stitching prevents fabric from stretching—when used with felt, it prevents both stretching and tearing.

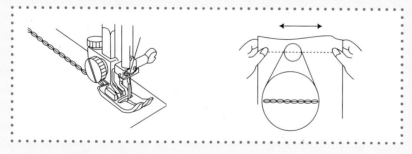

Stretch Stitch

This stitch is for sewing knits. Seams sewn with this stitch will not suffer from broken threads when stretched.

Appendix F: Hand and Embroidery Stitches

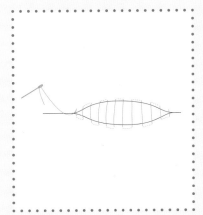

Ladder Stitch
Use the ladder stitch to close openings invisibly for a professional finish.

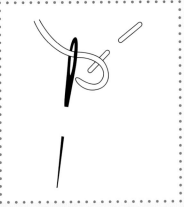

Running Stitch
Use this stitch with thread to join fabrics, or with ribbon, yarn or floss as a decorative element.

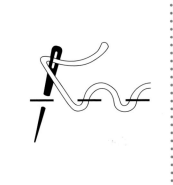

Threaded Running Stitch
Here's a way to add a decorative element to a simple running stitch.

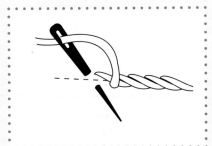

Stem Stitch
Perfect for making flowing, curved lines such as flower stems.

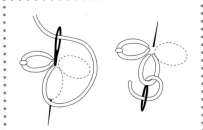

Lazy Daisy Stitch
Make a flower shape with loops for petals. The loops are held in place by the stitching.

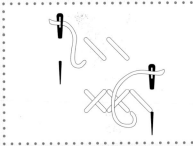

Cross Stitch
These traditional rows of X shapes make a pretty border.

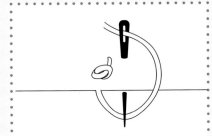

Blanket Stitch, Step 1
Knot the thread, insert the needle on the right side of the fabric near the edge, and exit on the wrong side.
** Bring the needle back up to the right side, then enter about ¼ inch from the edge. Exit on the wrong side, keeping your needle in front of the hanging thread.

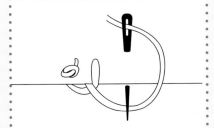

Blanket Stitch, Step 2
Repeat step 1 from **. Each stitch "traps" the hanging thread, forming a decorative edging.

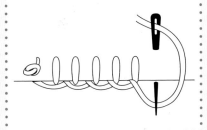

Blanket Stitch, Step 3
Keep going, and the pattern will emerge.

Index

Cloth Dolls

Brenda Brightmore

Create 10 beautiful cloth dolls in a range of styles! Contains easy-to-follow, full-size patterns, step-by-step photos and illustrations, and materials lists.

Paperback
128 pages
75 color photos
978-0-87349-871-5
0-87349-871-2
Item # CLDO

Fleecie Dolls

Fiona Goble

Create 15 cute, easy-to-sew friends from soft, cuddly fleece fabrics, using simple sewing and embroidery skills. Projects range from suitable for infants to cute and quirky for older children.

Paperback
112 pages
100 color illus.
978-0-89689-734-2
0-89689-734-6
Item # Z2816

Sew Baby Doll Clothes

Joan Hinds

Features 30+ projects and patterns for 12" to 22" dolls including pajamas, dresses, hats, blankets and more. Step-by-step instructions and color photos, and full-size patterns ensure sewing success.

Paperback
128 pages
50+ color photos, 175 illus.
978-0-87349-934-7
0-87349-934-4
Item # BDCA

Sew Today's Fashions for 18-Inch Dolls

Joan Hinds

Create the fashions children wear today, sized to fit your 18-inch dolls! This book contains over 50 easy-to-follow patterns.

Paperback
128 pages
75 color photos, 100+ illus.
978-0-87349-772-5
0-87349-772-4
Item # MCDF

Sew the Contemporary Wardrobe for 18-Inch Dolls

Joan Hinds

This fun book provides patterns for creating fashions for these ever-popular dolls.

Paperback
96 pages
50 color photos, 200+ illus.
978-0-87349-375-8
0-87349-375-3
Item # SCWD

These and other fine Krause Publications craft books are available at your local art & craft retailer, bookstore or online supplier or visit our website at:
www.mycraftivity.com